Praise for A C

'Immensely practical, tenderly compassionate and reassuringly conversational, this is the perfect companion for anyone experiencing loss. Full of lived wisdom, insights, suggestions and hope, it is above all shot through with kindness. Part guidebook, part instruction manual, part love letter, this is a book that takes you by the hand and promises the gentlest comfort in the darkest of times.'

TAMSIN GREIG, ACTOR

'Explaining how the mind and body work together, *A Grief Companion* offers insights into the process of grieving. The writing is energetic, down-to-earth and honest as Sasha Bates helps readers cope with the many layers and levels of grief. A useful as well as a moving book.'

CATHY RENTZENBRINK, AUTHOR OF *A MANUAL FOR HEARTACHE*

'This is the book I was searching for 20 years ago when my son died, thank heaven it exists now. It really is the perfect companion. It contains everything a bereaved person needs to piece together their new life without the person they loved. I will highly recommend it to my clients and to anyone accompanying a bereaved person through their grief.'

LIZZIE PICKERING, GRIEF INVESTIGATOR AND FILM AND PODCAST PRODUCER

'Sasha has put all her knowledge, as an experienced psychotherapist, and all her heart, as a woman grieving, into writing this book. It's a resource to treasure, and a great example of how to be kind to yourself from the midst of deep distress. It is beautifully laid out. I will certainly be using it in my practice and recommending it to clients who have suffered loss.'

TOIREASA MCCANN, PSYCHOTHERAPIST

'Sasha Bates draws on her work as a psychotherapist and her own personal experiences of loss to offer a flexible and holistic toolkit to bring comfort and hope to anyone whose life has been shattered by grief. Structured into sections on mind, body, spirit and the everyday, this new book is packed full of useful insights and resources – from vocabulary lists that help you pinpoint and communicate your emotions, to advice about funerals, relationships, anniversaries, and a range of therapeutic and creative activities. *A Grief Companion* will act as both a compassionate friend and an expert mentor on your grief journey, enabling you to manage life after loss in a way that is right for you.'

DR LESEL DAWSON, UNIVERSITY OF BRISTOL AND ARTS AND CULTURE LEAD OF THE GOOD GRIEF FESTIVAL

A Grief Companion

Practical support and a
guiding hand through
the darkness of loss

Sasha Bates

First published in Great Britain in 2021 by Yellow Kite
An Imprint of Hodder & Stoughton

An Hachette UK company

1

Copyright © Sasha Bates 2021

The right of Sasha Bates to be identified as the Author of the Work
has been asserted by her in accordance with the Copyright,
Designs and Patents Act 1988.

Text Design by Goldust Design
Illustrations from shutterstock.com

A CIP catalogue record for this title is available from the British Library

Trade Paperback ISBN 978 1 529 34360 1
eBook ISBN 978 1 529 34361 8

Typeset in Minion by Goldust Design

Printed and bound in Great Britain by Clays Ltd, Elcograf S.p.A.

Hodder & Stoughton policy is to use papers that are natural, renewable
and recyclable products and made from wood grown in sustainable forests.
The logging and manufacturing processes are expected to conform to the
environmental regulations of the country of origin.

Yellow Kite
Hodder & Stoughton Ltd
Carmelite House
50 Victoria Embankment
London EC4Y 0DZ

www.yellowkitebooks.co.uk

For my husband, Bill Cashmore, my father, Peter Bates, and my uncle, Mervyn Woolliams – amazing men whom I adore, and whose untimely deaths have taught me so much about the varied shapes and flavours of grief.

Introduction

My husband Bill died, and I wrote a book about it. You may have read that book. That book might be the reason you are now reading this one. Not that it matters either way, but if you did you will know that I don't believe there are easy ways to shortcut the pain of grief, nor that it is something that you ever 'get over'. It is a truly horrible and long-lasting experience and I can't pretend it is not.

But wait, please don't stop reading – it's not all as gloomy and depressing as that last sentence makes it sound. There are many things that make it more bearable – for me writing the book was one of them, as was reading other people's books on the subject, or, at times, books that were very far from the subject. And I have certainly had, and hopefully will continue to have, many moments of joy and lightness and pleasure in my life since Bill died, despite my ongoing grief and sadness over losing him. But I can't talk about those nice moments without first acknowledging that the backdrop to it all is awful, and painful, and not an experience that any of us would ever voluntarily choose to undergo. And that's just the thing – we don't volunteer for it, we don't choose it, yet this horrible thing will happen to every single one of us. It may not be a spouse that you lose, but you will lose parents, friends or siblings, and even, if you are really unlucky, a child, or perhaps an unborn child. That being the case, this book would like to serve as a companion to you as you journey through your own grief, whomever it is for.

This book gives you permission to do your grief, your way. I'm not here to claim that I have got it 'right', which would be impossible, nor can I offer any definitive answers as to the best ways of managing the pain. But what I can offer are suggestions as to how you might go about finding what those ways might be – for you. I can only do that by telling you of some of the things I have found useful, and that others have told me they found useful, and by leaving the space – metaphorically, but also literally in the case of the white spaces you will find herein – for you to add your own ideas, experiences, feelings, lists, doodles, coffee cup or tear stains. You may also find it useful to buy yourself a nice notebook in which to expand more fully on some of those suggestions, and into which you can paste your own pictures, mementoes, poems, quotes, or anything else that you discover along the way and from which you derive strength, comfort or inspiration.

You can try my suggestions – or not. And you may find them helpful – or not. Any or all of those responses are fine. You are going through one of the worst and most difficult experiences of your life and neither I nor anyone else can tell you the best way for you to do that. You know yourself better than the rest of us ever can, so you do it your way. If some of what follows helps you to find what that way is, then I am delighted to have been able to offer you some small respite from the horror, even if just for a few moments. It may not feel like it now, but those moments will get longer and more frequent, while the horrible ones will get shorter and less frequent. That may take some time, however.

My aim for this book is that it might, in its own small way, help encourage that shift in ratios to inch ahead faster. I also hope that it might, eventually, offer some optimism to let you know that you will find light and courage from out of this darkness, and you will be transformed by it. Your grief will not leave you, but you will arrange yourself around it differently. However unwillingly you entered into this, you will find some good things emerging in time. Maybe not today, maybe not even this year, but one day.

I also hope that if you are the friend of a bereaved person this book will provide a small glimpse into the complexity of what your friend could be going through. It will hopefully generate some clues and ideas as to what they may need from you; and there's a section, very near the end, aimed just at you as well. You can support your friend on their journey by thinking about some of the suggestions in this book, and pondering which could be helpful, and which may be less so. But more important than the practicalities is if you can take on board the book's central message, which is that your friend's grief is unique to them and they will need to feel their way through it in their own way, and at their own pace. It is not your job to tell them what you think they should be doing at any point, nor to pass comment or judgement if you would like them to be doing it differently. Try to support them at the place where they are, not push them to where you would like them to be. Follow, don't lead, and if you do happen to proffer any of the suggestions herein make sure it is just that – an offer not an instruction.

This book does not need to be read in any sort of order because grief is not linear and what feels helpful at one point may feel unhelpful at others. Mood swings are an inherent characteristic of grief, so allow yourself to take it all one step at a time and know that what you need from day to day will change. And change again. To give you a little guidance as to where to begin, however, the book is separated into different sections so you can see which might speak to you at any one time. Those sections are:

MIND – for when you want to engage the brain and think about what is going on for you;

BODY – for when your physical self is dominating your responses;

SPIRIT – for when you are feeling more reflective and pondering the bigger questions;

EVERYDAY – for when there is nothing for it but to engage with paperwork and washing-up and the other mundanities of life, both the familiar, and all those myriad extra tasks thrown up by a death. There are also a few bits and pieces that you may want to dip into when necessary – about Christmas, anniversaries and triggers for instance – and some lists of resources that might offer support. There is also a section here that you may want to show those friends who would like to help you but don't know how.

So, choose which area feels right for you to start with today, or just open the book at random and see what awaits you there. I wish you luck. I am also sending you love and the hope that this book will serve as a friend and companion alongside you on this horrible experience you are undertaking so unwillingly.

Mind

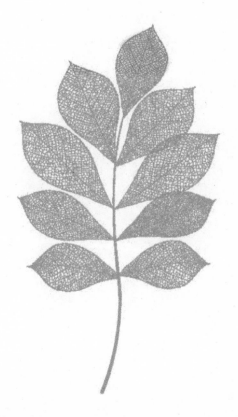

Grief really messes with your mind. Not only are you stuck in the grip of unfamiliar and intense emotions, but you are likely to be cycling through them rapidly and while feeling unable to control either the intensity or the speed of the change. You are likely to be feeling very confused, very unstable and very foggy. Panicky even. You may be struggling to make even simple decisions, you may be forgetful, inarticulate, slow, or struggling with any number of unusual symptoms – see page 16 for just some of these.

There are many reasons for this, which we will look at later. The most important thing is that you both understand that it is completely normal, and try to forgive yourself and handle yourself gently during this time. My advice is to treat yourself as you would an unruly toddler who is governed by their immediate needs and wants, and whose brain is not yet formed enough to be able to mediate or regulate those overpowering feelings. That toddler – and you right now – needs calm, careful, compassionate handling. They do not need judgement, to be told to pull themselves together, or criticism. Nor do you need to see this as a sign of madness, or that you will never again regain your faculties as you know them. This is temporary and will pass. But while it is there, proceed gently and kindly.

Or you may be feeling perplexed by grief and the very notion of 'accessing' emotions might seem alien. You may feel completely numb, or slightly removed from it all, and as if you don't really 'get' what others are talking about when they describe such discombobulation. You may find 'thinking' about it to be a useful route into understanding on an intellectual level. We all respond differently, and I hope that there may be something in here for everyone.

What follows are some suggestions as to what might help on any given day. There will be days when you want to distract from the pain and attempt some semblance of normal life, and then others when you really need to go inside your pain, feel it, acknowledge it, and allow those emotions to be experienced and expressed. Likewise there will be days when you have lots of energy and want to get on and do things and look outward and forward, and days when you feel like you've been hit by a bus and have no energy even to get dressed, let alone be productive; days when you need to fold inward and just focus on getting through the next breath. This book keeps all of those pairs of opposites in mind and offers ideas to address both sides of their contradictory nature. So pick your day and your mood. Do/don't do. Distract/immerse. Challenge yourself/indulge yourself. Learn to allow and accept your changing moods and energy levels and work with them, not against them. You have experienced a traumatic event and you need time to adapt, and you need to treat yourself kindly at this time of vulnerability and change.

You may also want to use these intense moods and adaptations as an opportunity to get to know yourself better; to use them as tools from which to learn about your automatic responses and your innate tendencies. You may discover when these can be useful, and when they are less so. Grief, with all its intensity and pain and terror, can actually be a time of immense growth; a time when you learn about yourself and all that you are capable of. It teaches you that you can survive the worst. But you may need to go deeper into 'the worst' in order to come through it. If that idea horrifies you then ignore it and move to another part of the book. You may return to it many moons hence, or never. That's all fine – this is absolutely not a book intent on telling you how to be. It's a book to support you with where you are now and potentially offer hope that things can change.

So try the suggestions you like, ignore the ones you don't. Grief is not one-size-fits-all and if some of them don't speak to you, that doesn't mean you are doing it wrong; it just means you are doing it your way, and that is not only fine, but necessary.

Here are just some
of the symptoms of grief
that can affect the mind:

Brain fog   Confusion

Forgetfulness

Feeling that nothing makes sense

Inability to concentrate

Searching for reasons

Searching for distractions

Denial   Disbelief   Minimisation

Lack of purpose

Out of control   Helplessness

Searching for purpose   Madness

Not recognising yourself

Anxiety   Depression   Hopelessness

Panic attacks   Overwhelm

Hyper-vigilance

Find Words

So much of grief feels inexpressible. We have a cultural taboo around death itself, which silences many, while expressing condolences or knowing how to talk to grievers leaves some feeling tongue-tied. We, the grievers, often feel so stirred up and emotionally confused that mere words cannot adequately convey that tumult. Yet somehow finding ways to express our emotion can feel very freeing and help make sense of some of it. A bit like an old Polaroid picture slowly becoming visible as it develops.

Metaphor

My book *Languages of Loss*, written in the wake of my husband Bill's death, explored some of my ways of making that fuzzy picture clearer in order to unpick and care for my ever-changing feelings. Some of those 'languages' weren't verbal at all – I found things like movement, art and music often said it better than words could and you will find much more about these other modes of expression in the later sections on Body and Spirit. But I found that using words slightly more laterally, more obscurely, helped too. I experimented with metaphor, imagery, visualisations, myth, storytelling and poetry – trialling as many ways as I could to verbalise what often felt unverbalisable. Some of these I came up with myself, sometimes I needed to allow others to do it for me. The poem by Rumi that ends this chapter is one that expressed my truth more precisely than I was able to do myself.

Vocabulary

Feelings in particular are hard to decipher, especially if we don't have the vocabulary. We fall back on familiar but not very descriptive stalwarts – 'I feel rubbish, angry, confused, a bit down'. Trying to name things more precisely would be useful but we need to expand our emotional vocabulary to do that. On page 21 is an 'inventory of feelings' – a selection of descriptive words that might help you narrow down more precisely what you may be feeling at any one time. You can of course write your own in your notebook as well. I've focused only on the uncomfortable feelings but if you feel the need – and I hope often you do – you can look online for the plethora of happier, more welcome and more comfortable feelings too, for when you are able to explore the return of those. And return they will, in time, even if that feels hard to believe right now.

Multiple meanings

One final word on words. Well, a few final words on words actually. Sometimes the same word can mean very different things to different people and it's important that you know what you mean by each. For me, it is another one of the reasons why I wanted to write *Languages of Loss* and why I tried to choose my words so carefully and give ownership of them over to the reader, not keep them just for myself.

What do I mean by all that? Well, take the word 'survive' for instance, which is one that gets bandied about a lot in grief and which I get asked about a lot. How does one survive a grief so excruciatingly painful? To some this word evokes only negativity. Is life after bereavement so hard and bare that it is just about surviving? Is the image conjured up that of an emaciated and lonely castaway grappling around a desert island, eating insects to keep death at bay? Does this image suggest a stark life, one in which you just do what you can to not die, while clinging to a life that isn't really worth having anyway, such is its meagreness and hardness? Is that what survival means to you? If so, then it will not be a notion you want to dwell on.

And yet there is another reading of it, which may be what other people mean. And that is not allowing oneself to be pushed under or squashed by it. No one listening to Gloria Gaynor belt out her totemic anthem will be under any illusions that her rallying cry of 'I will survive' means anything other than that she will thrive and go on to do bigger and better things as a result of the agony of her loss.

Neither reading is right or wrong. Well, they are both right to someone and wrong to someone else. What I am saying is make sure you know which it is to you, and use the word in that way, and if someone uses it in the opposite way and that doesn't land well with you, then clarify that their words are not helpful and you prefer your interpretation. This is true of any of those 'grief' words that get bandied about so carelessly and which have the power to conversely wound or soothe. By drilling down into what you really mean by each word, I think you can discover your own feelings a bit more intensely, and so render that

Polaroid's focus a little sharper. You can create a way of surviving that becomes truly yours.

Make words your friends

Find a word for your feelings

apprehensive dread foreboding frightened
mistrustful panicked petrified scared suspicious
terrified wary worried anxious alarmed
nervous timid shaky restless doubtful threatened
cowardly quaking menaced small vulnerable

aggravated dismayed disgruntled displeased
exasperated frustrated impatient irritated irked
enraged furious incensed indignant irate hostile
insulted sore upset hateful unpleasant
offended bitter livid outraged resentful
aggressive inflamed provoked infuriated cross
worked-up boiling fuming shaken fizzing

animosity appalled contempt disgusted
aversion hatred horrified hostile repulsed
loathing repugnance distaste
antipathy abhorrence detestation

ambivalent baffled bewildered dazed hesitant

lost mystified perplexed puzzled torn

upset doubtful uncertain indecisive

embarrassed unlike self shy

stupefied unbelieving sceptical distrustful

misgiving unsure uneasy

pessimistic dismayed

alienated aloof apathetic bored

cold detached distant distracted indifferent

numb removed uninterested withdrawn low down

not myself disinterested lifeless preoccupied

agitated

alarmed discombobulated disconcerted

disturbed perturbed rattled restless shocked

startled surprised troubled turbulent

turmoil uncomfortable uneasy

unnerved unsettled

upset preoccupied cold

ashamed chagrined flustered guilty
mortified self-conscious

beat burnt out depleted exhausted lethargic
listless sleepy tired weary worn out bored
insensitive neutral

Agonised appalled humiliated wronged alienated
anguished bereaved devastated
grief heartbroken hurt
lonely miserable regretful remorseful crushed
tormented deprived pained tortured dejected
rejected injured offended afflicted
aching victimised

depressed dejected despair despondent
disappointed discouraged disheartened
forlorn gloomy heavy-hearted hopeless
melancholy unhappy wretched lousy ashamed
powerless diminished miserable detestable
sulky agonised bad hurt

anxious cranky distressed distraught edgy
fidgety frazzled irritable jittery nervous
overwhelmed restless stressed out
tense annoyed

fragile guarded helpless insecure leery reserved
sensitive shaky abandoned wrangled

envious jealous longing nostalgic pining wistful
empty seeking heartbroken

Start a journal

Fill your paper with the breathings of your heart
WORDSWORTH

There have been a lot of studies into the benefits of journaling during grief. Harvard University research has shown that putting your deepest emotions down on paper can work simultaneously on physical and emotional health, boosting your immune system alongside your mood and motivation. Conversely, holding feelings in can increase blood pressure, heart rate and muscle tension. Their research into journaling also shows that it works best if you do it regularly over the course of several days as opposed to just trying it once, so if you do give it a go, keep at it for a while.

There are many things that may put you off journaling – you may feel intimidated, have no motivation or energy, not know what to write. But my advice is to just start writing anything, even if it doesn't make sense, and soon it might start to. Here's some reasons why. And some 'hows'.

- Grief can be hard to put into words, not just to others but even to ourselves. But leaving all those confusing, contradictory, tumultuous thoughts racing around madly in our heads can make us feel just that – mad. Trying to get something down on paper can be a way of making some sort of sense of it all.

- Put all ideas of trying to create something 'good' out of your mind. Just write and keep at it without any thought for the end result. Even write nonsense. It really doesn't matter – no one else will ever see it (unless you want them to). It's just a way of getting some of the intangible mass of words and feelings out from inside you and on to something more external and tangible like a notebook or screen.

If freeform journaling feels too unbounded and intimidating, write it in the form of a letter. That might be a letter to the person who has died. It might be a letter to yourself, or a younger version of yourself, or an older version of yourself. It might be a letter that you wish your dead loved one could write to you.

If you feel you really can't write a journal, then you could do something more comfortable or familiar to you:

Send an email to a friend, writing about the person who has died as though describing them to someone who didn't know them, or as though you've been asked by imaginary (or real) future grandchildren what they were like.

If you really feel you can't write at all, then think about other modes of expression that maybe come more easily to you – like a voice memo, or a video diary.

Whichever way you do it, do try to express your pain in some way – it lightens the internal turmoil and can help clarify and reveal. We cannot all be – in fact none of us can be – Shakespeare, but as he said so eloquently in *Macbeth*:

Give sorrow words; the grief that does not speak knits up the o-er wrought heart and bids it break.

SO TODAY'S SUGGESTION IS:

Write about it

Buy a notebook and start jotting down thoughts and feelings as you think of them or when the mood strikes.

Journaling: the benefits

It can help improve physical health – research has shown that release of energy brings physical benefits and reduces stress and its effects.

It can help improve mental health – it has been shown to reduce both depression and anxiety.

It can improve sleep – a bit like the 'worry dolls' given to children, getting your thoughts out before bedtime can stop them circulating around in your head and stopping you sleeping.

If you find it hard to talk to others about how you are feeling, then your journal can offer a non-judgemental, always-available, friendly ear – one that you don't have to worry about boring or overwhelming.

Prepare to Do Nothing

There are going to be days when you literally can't do anything. When the pain is so huge you are doubled over in agony, when the horror and fear stop you breathing and you fear for your survival, when the hopelessness is so overwhelming you cannot lift your head from the pillow, or the howls and sobs are so all-consuming that you fear you will never stop or be able to face the world ever again. Those days will come, and you won't have the energy to pick up this book, let alone engage with any of the suggestions in it.

On days like that you can't really help but give in to the feelings and go with it. But I do have one suggestion. Given that when in the grip of those feelings you won't be able to fight them, what you can do instead is to do a bit of emotional stockpiling in advance for when these days hit. You can fill your literal and your metaphorical cupboards with enough props to get you through the siege. Perhaps, just perhaps, a bit of preparation might alleviate a tiny fraction of the pain. These are my suggestions:

- Choose your most trusted and understanding friend and have them on standby (see page 31).

- Have a cupboard or freezer full of comfort food. When you don't have the energy to shop or prepare meals, you will at least know that with minimal effort you can turn to your stockpiles of soup or porridge, ice cream or chocolate, popcorn or whatever else it is that you crave when in the depths of despair.

- Don't make too many plans in advance, and any you do make, only agree to things with the proviso that you may have to pull out at the last minute, or may need to leave early, maybe even without warning.

- Have a favourite playlist of music or meditations or inspirational talks or podcasts to listen to.

- If you have children, have someone ready to look after them for you.

SO TODAY'S SUGGESTION IS:

Plan ahead for the bad days

Reflect on the things you would like to do in preparation for the bad days that you know will come.

Finding a trusted friend

Do you have a friend who can be relied on just to listen? Someone who doesn't feel the need to give advice or want to 'solve'; who is robust enough not to fall apart if you do, yet sympathetic and sensitive enough to understand that the tears need to keep coming?

Once identified, put that friend on standby for the really bad days. Warn them that there will be times when you can't be with people, but you also can't be alone. At those times they need to be ready at the end of the phone.

Warn them that in that phone call you may be too upset even to form words, but that you just need to be able to sob or breathe or fall asleep listening to the sound of someone else breathing alongside, even over the airwaves.

Prepping this friend in advance alleviates the need to explain all the above while in the middle of a crisis that has you unable to form a sentence, let alone articulate your need. Someone hearing your pain helps you feel less alone in the agony.

Ask your friend to prep others on your behalf too. If people are forewarned that you are fragile and unreliable – justifiably so – you give yourself an escape route without needing to feel guilty. Buying yourself the space to collapse can take away some of the pressure that builds when you are not feeling up to doing something you feel you ought to do – because pressure is more likely to provoke the collapse in the first place.

Know Your Audience

Different friends and family members have different skills and can be helpful in different ways.

- Some are great **listeners** and will be good to be with when you just need to talk and cry.

- Some are great **solvers**. They won't be able to just listen without wanting to find a 'solution', which may be upsetting when you need to talk and really be in your feelings. So, don't ask them to be something they are not. Instead know you can turn to these people when you feel you need help in getting something done, when you've had enough (for the moment) of crying and emoting, and just want to know how to sort out the bank accounts or redirect mail, or when you need help with car insurance or walking the dog.

- Some will be great at making you **laugh**. There will be many times when you don't want to be 'jollied along', when you want your pain to be heard and acknowledged. But there will be other times when you need a break from all the suffering and prefer to be distracted by having a good laugh.

- Some are great **talkers**. When you want to be reminded of your dead loved one, or just want a gentle and undemanding soundtrack that will take the pressure off you to perform, then let this person tell you stories and drift off into nostalgia.

Some will be great at **childcare** and can take the children off your hands, or will know how to play with or occupy them when you need a break.

SO TODAY'S SUGGESTION IS:

Think about who is good at what

Reflect on which friends you would like to call in which situations.

Change Up Your Routines and Habits

As with so many things in grief, you may find returning to your regular routines and habits to be either comforting or painful. And you won't always know in advance which it will be.

Sometimes I found watching comedies on television comforting because I knew how much Bill liked me to laugh, and I could also imagine hearing him laugh at the things I knew he found funny. Other times it was deeply painful as it highlighted that I would never again hear his astute comments and observations about the shows we used to watch together.

I found continuing to attend my weekly Quaker Meeting very comforting. Not because I felt better when I got there – often in fact I felt worse, as I had all that space and time to think about Bill and so the sadness and tears would pour forth – but because it was a return to something that we had started doing together, and I could very easily feel his presence on the bench next to me as I sat there.

Other routines just floored me, and I had to completely change my usual way of doing things. The first time I went back to the cinema I realised that doing the same thing, but without him, just highlighted his absence in too painful a way and I cried throughout the supposed comedy. I realised I needed to go to a different cinema that held fewer memories, where I would be forced into creating new habits and routines where I wasn't always comparing being with him to being without him.

Change it up

Write a list of which habits are comforting, and which are triggering, then jot down some ideas for how to do the painful ones differently. For instance:

- See friends in different environments.

- If you always used to go to the same pub or restaurant with the same people, then go with a different group of people, or make sure it's not just couples or families or whatever dynamic most triggers you.

- Or meet at a different time of day.

- Or meet in a different restaurant.

- Shop in different shops or buy different types of food.

- Sit at a different place at the table.

- Swap to the other side of the bed.

- Take a different route or mode of transport to work.

- Get your lunch from a different cafe.

🍃 If you used to go to the gym together, move to a different gym or take up a different activity once you get there.

🍃 Or change the time of day you go there.

The glaring absence can be made so apparent by doing the same things you used to do but with a hole where your loved one once was. Changing practical things may help lessen some of that pain.

Create a Legacy

Finding ways to keep your loved one's memory alive can be a very important part of grieving. In the early days this may involve lots of talking about them, reminiscing, hearing other people tell you stories about them – ones you already know, others that may be new. That can – and should – of course last long beyond the early days, but for now it may be all you have.

Make it clear to your friends that you like hearing their name mentioned – if indeed that is something you do like. Otherwise people may well avoid the subject for fear of 'upsetting' you. They need to know that the opposite is true, that mentioning their name shows how loved the person was, and how that is therefore comforting.

I found that by bringing up Bill's name first, and early on in a conversation, it made other people relax – they no longer had to check themselves for fear of saying the wrong thing.

When the early shock has passed you may want to do something more concrete to keep their memory alive. This can range from the very small to the elaborate – it doesn't matter what it is, as long as it serves the purpose of you having something to remember them by that goes beyond just your own memories or words. The obvious and time-worn example of this is, of course, creating a headstone for a grave, and keeping it well tended with flowers, but there are many other things you can do if that doesn't feel appropriate or if you want to do something additional.

One of the things that I have done to memorialise Bill is to set up a scholarship in his name – The Bill Cashmore Award – which enables a young theatre-maker to create a play. This scholarship provides not just money, but also training, mentorship and resources with which to create an original, socially conscious and entertaining piece of theatre, and is run in conjunction with my local theatre, the Lyric Hammersmith. My background in the media, and Bill's background in the theatre, mean that this was an obvious choice for me, and many of our friends have been able to offer masterclasses and workshops as well as funding. I mention this because your way of memorialising doesn't necessarily have to involve money, if that is difficult for you. It could be much broader in scope – think of people like Baroness Doreen Lawrence OBE, who campaigns to get institutional racism in the police recognised and tackled after the death of her son, Stephen.

Memorialising can of course be far smaller in scale, but no less meaningful in impact.

For instance:

- Throw a party on a significant date such as their birthday or organise a group walk to a special place that meant something to them.

- Have a plaque installed on a park bench or a theatre seat, or at their local football stadium.

- Donate some trees to the Woodland Trust so that you have a specific area of woodland to visit, knowing it wouldn't be there if it wasn't for your person.

- Plant a tree in your own garden or local park – if allowed. Or simply plant a flower or plant in your front room or in a window box. The size or ambition really don't matter – something small in size but which you see every day, and which changes with the seasons and the light, can remind you that your person is still with you in other ways.

- Fundraise for one of their favourite charities – when my friend Richard Garrett died at the age of just 51, his friends and family set about raising money for charities he had supported. This evolved naturally, garnering the name 'Challenge 51' with the aim of raising £51,000. It involved a whole series of sponsored events, culminating in his wife Emma hiking up Mount Kenya with a group of friends – something Richard himself had done many years earlier.

- Have their ashes made into a piece of jewellery or put them inside a piece of sculpture. Or simply do as I did with Bill's wedding ring – I put it on the chain of an existing necklace so as to keep him close to my heart always.

- When my father died my niece, Isobel, had the idea to turn a pair of his cufflinks into necklaces for me, my mother, my sister and herself and we all wear these matching necklaces on significant days – or just when we feel we want him close to us. Which is often.

- Create a memory box to preserve any little mementoes that remind you of the person, including examples of their handwriting or sketches, and of course photos. Having something physical and tactile that you can touch can be more comforting than just seeing these things digitally.

- Create a ritual – this can be absolutely anything you want it to be. You could possibly dedicate a special night every year on which you and friends get together to make your person's favourite food, or go to their favourite restaurant and reminisce, tell anecdotes and stories about the person. You could even make up a quiz based on their lives, or a bingo game based on their funny sayings with some of their possessions as prizes. Or the ritual could be smaller and more private, something like lighting a candle and looking through photos on your own.

- Create a memorial website where you can gather together bits of information that others can add to, possibly even a forum where people can chat together.

SO TODAY'S SUGGESTION IS:

Keep their name alive

List a few things your loved one liked or was interested in, or some charities they supported. Something in there might one day give you an idea for a way of memorialising them. Meanwhile find time to occasionally lose yourself in photos and reminiscences, ask friends to write down a memory or unearth a photo, and think about the smaller ripples your loved one created – how they affected others and the world around them.

Communicate

How and with whom you communicate will very much depend on what both you, and your friends, can bear. That may take you by surprise and it may take a bit of experimentation for you to work out how best to get the support you need.

Some friends will be filled with terror at possibly saying the wrong thing, of 'upsetting' you, making things worse. Others will be afraid that interacting with you will bring up fears about confronting their own mortality. Some may avoid you completely so as to avoid their embarrassment.

So you may need to help them to help you. Because you will need them.

Most people really want to help, they just don't know how. And you may not know how to ask for help, or what kind of help you need.

Be honest
Experiment with giving friends a true glimpse into how unsure and wobbly you feel. Open up about how sometimes you may want to chat and be 'normal', while sometimes talking feels too much so although you would like them there with you, you would prefer a quiet, even silent, presence.

Be direct
Most people quite like the straightforwardness of being told what to do. It takes the pressure off their awkwardness and makes them feel useful.

Don't shield them

If you are really struggling for money or are worried about losing your home then let them know just how bad things are; they may have more lateral ideas as to how to address the reality of your situation.

Let them be useful

If there are jobs that you know need doing, however random they may seem, then just ask, safe in the knowledge that friends will be so relieved at having a job to do that you can pretty much get away with anything! It's one of the very few perks of this awful time, so make the most of it. Joking aside, you do need to help them to help you, if you can.

Be aware of the flipside

While other people can be the best resource you have to get through this, at the same time they can be the cause of pain. I found that I couldn't bear to be alone; I needed other people around to hug me and show me that I had support and was still loved. But even though they were all my best friends, they nevertheless also highlighted Bill's absence even more. No matter how hard they tried, they couldn't replace him. Nothing was as fun as it would be with him, they weren't as witty or as easy to be with as him, and of course there wasn't the casualness of living in the same house and knowing each other inside out. Bill and I didn't need to talk or be in the same room, and we certainly didn't have to 'entertain' each other in the same way you do with friends, however good a friend they are. It took some practice, but the more I was able to convey just how contradictory and ever-changing my moods and needs were, and the more I was able to help them see that these were not about them, but just about the grief, the easier it became.

Expand your network

Conversely, you may not know enough people who are offering to help. And when you are in the grip of grief you have probably never felt less able to reach out and find friends. But there are ways of asking for help even when it is not offered.

Ask the friends you do have to spread the word and galvanise others. Look what happened during the coronavirus lockdown – WhatsApp groups sprang up immediately and people were falling over themselves to help others, even those they barely knew.

Use professionals

Lawyers, celebrants, religious leaders and therapists are there to help with more specific expertise. It's not the same as having friends around, but what they may lack in intimacy they make up for with experience. They are used to talking to the bereaved and do tend to know who's who in the community, so can help find you more informal help; and some people may even become friends in time. There is nothing like getting to know someone during your darkest hour for forging strong bonds. People you meet at this time of vulnerability may very well turn out to be lifelong friends. As with my quip about perks earlier, there are gems to be found in the rubble of grief – connecting with people more deeply than ever before can be one of them.

Find a community

Getting to know others who have been through something similar to what you are going through can serve many purposes:

It can normalise some of what you are feeling so you feel less mad and alone (I'm projecting out how I felt in the early days – you may feel neither of those things);

It can provide companions to walk alongside you on your path who will act as a guiding hand and pick you up when you trip;

It can show you that others have survived, even though they too once felt that survival was impossible, as you may do now;

They can offer a space where you may feel safe to share just how bad you feel, knowing you will be understood and that no one will try to 'solve' or minimise you.

Never forget, however, that your grief is still yours and is unique to you and, while others can help shine a light on the path, your path is yours alone and no one can know exactly how you feel or what you need. See the resources list at the end of the book for groups and support groups you can turn to such as Cruse, Way and The Good Grief Project.

Be careful

There is another category of people, who need rather more careful handling. People whom I rather callously call 'grief tourists' and whom I've also heard called 'grief junkies'. People who aren't particularly good friends, but who suddenly want to be around you all the time, who just want to be part of the grief, at the centre of the drama. Often they need to show you how much they are grieving, need you to see how upset they are, maybe even want to be comforted by you. Others may do all the right things at the time, but later seem to feel justified in 'calling in a debt'. They want to remind you how good they were to you and for you to show what they deem to be the right amount of gratitude and payback. They take advantage of your darkest hour to aggrandise themselves and make themselves out to be the hero of the hour, your rescuer. Sadly it isn't always easy to spot who these people might be, but if a person who you don't normally see much of is suddenly very present, or if someone feels a bit too pushy and intrusive, then this might be a good indicator. You can gently back off if you get a sense this is happening – your all-too-real grief is a good excuse to say you don't feel up to seeing anyone beyond your closest circle right now; or you could enlist one of those trusted, close friends to act as a bit of a gatekeeper for you.

SO MY FIRST SUGGESTION FOR TODAY IS:

Communicate

... whether to friends or strangers – even if all you are communicating is your lack of ability to communicate.

AND MY SECOND SUGGESTION FOR TODAY

Be careful

... you are in a very fragile state and you do need to only spend time with people who respect your vulnerability. You are allowed to say no to help and company as well as being allowed to say yes to it.

Engage the Brain

There were days when I felt my mind had turned to mush, when even the simplest tasks were completely beyond me – I couldn't remember how to drive a car or put the washing machine on. I couldn't remember the names of simple household objects. My body was just one heaving, weeping mess with seemingly no functioning brain attached. I didn't want to – couldn't – think about how little I was able to think. My brain was not my own and I just wanted to ignore it and immerse myself in my feelings.

At other times I couldn't bear being stuck within that physical and emotional pain any longer and needed to reacquaint myself with the fact that I was once a functioning human being. I needed my brain to come back online and tell me what on Earth was going on, to explain to me that all this was normal, and give me some theory and context to help me understand why I was feeling so weirdly unlike myself. I wanted to find out what others had said about the experience, to understand the universals, learn how others had survived.

Sometimes I hated the thought that others had felt what I was feeling because it felt so unique to me, and to Bill, and to our relationship. It felt special and as though no one else could ever understand, and I didn't want to know how others had done it because they weren't us. So sometimes I wanted to read more therapeutically and get into the part of the brain that could observe objectively and analytically – not to see how universal my suffering was and to understand it as normal, but instead to look at my unique make-up and understand what was individual to me that was causing my particular responses; to create some space, and in a way rise above the experience by trying to understand what it was in my background, temperament and childhood that was causing me to respond in my own particular way.

Other times I just wanted to lose myself in being efficient and organised – addressing the paperwork, sorting out the bank accounts, cancelling the memberships, doing filing.

Grief can be so, so lonely. You are out of step with everyone around you and the difficulty of being able to communicate, share, know that others understand is part of what makes it so traumatic. Reading a good book on grief and hearing of others' experience can help rewrite your own narrative, reframing it as something that is part of a larger whole.

SO TODAY'S SUGGESTION IS:

Engage the brain

See if you can get some distance from the 'how' it is feeling, by understanding 'why' it feels that way.

On page 48 are some suggestions for reading material (there are plenty of others too) that might help you to get some understanding of what is going on for you and why it hurts as it does.

Suggested Reading

By therapists:

Sasha Bates – *Languages of Loss*

Julia Samuel – *Grief Works*

Megan Devine – *It's OK That You're Not OK*

Elizabeth Harper Neeld – *Seven Choices: Finding Daylight After Loss Shatters Your World*

Therese A. Rando – *How to Go on Living When Someone You Love Dies*

George A. Bonanno – *The Other Side of Sadness*

David Kessler – *Finding Meaning*

Zoë Clark-Coates – *Beyond Goodbye*

Memoirs:

C. S. Lewis – *A Grief Observed*

Decca Aitkenhead – *All at Sea*

Julian Barnes – *Levels of Life*

Take Control of What You Can

Death takes away your control and your sense of stability. And there is little that feels worse than uncertainty – I think living through lockdown showed us all that. So focus on what you can do, not on what you can't. Focus on the next hour, not the next day or week or month. Certainly not the next year. You will not always feel this helpless, foggy and out of control, so big decisions can wait till you feel stronger. If all you feel able to focus on right now is making the next cup of tea, then do that and feel pleased with your achievement once you have done it. Celebrating minor successes is also part of taking control, even when those successes might have seemed minor to your pre-bereavement self – making, or even eating, a meal, for instance.

Do not rush it, but there will be a time when you feel up to a slightly higher level of functioning than those just mentioned. And when that time comes, then there are some practical things that will help you feel more on top, and that is really important. When so much of your life feels as if it's been taken out of your control, reminding yourself what you can still take control of is empowering and reduces anxiety.

Research has shown that life can feel a bit more manageable if you stick to a simple daily schedule. In the early days this may be as simple as *have a shower, get dressed, get downstairs*, but as the weeks go by you can add other tasks to your day. Having a schedule not only breaks up the interminable days and forces you to change state occasionally, but it also takes away the need for decisions – you don't have to think about whether you want to get out for a walk or phone your friend, you just have to follow the simple tasks allocated to you.

- Break your day down into manageable chunks of time, create a timetable and stick to it. Be very specific with your planning so as to regain that feeling of control.

- If at all possible start by committing to getting up, going to bed and eating meals at the same time every day.

- Include slots in the timetable for the things that you have to do – like chores and housework – but keep these short and manageable.

- Build in slots for things that you know will help your mental and physical health, like exercise – even if it's just a short walk – as well as something more reflective or meditative that can help you feel absorbed in the moment.

- Schedule in time for communicating with friends – definitely make sure you speak to at least one person at least once a day even if you don't feel like it. If that's hard, ask your friends to call you at what you know is the hardest part of the day to get through.

- Engage in self-care, whatever that means to you – a bath, a massage, a walk (and see the Spirit section).

🌿 Most importantly, have time allocated each day for something that makes you feel some sort of pleasure. It might be tiny at the moment – it might be stroking the cat, eating chocolate, lighting a candle, knitting. The options are obviously endless but find the thing that makes your heart lift, even if only for a moment. Sticking to a timetable does require discipline, but disciplining yourself even the tiniest amount is also a form of taking control and that can feel empowering.

🌿 Getting organised around the house can also feed the sense of being in control – of your immediate environment at least – and it seems also to satisfy a sort of nesting instinct that can often arise in the wake of a bereavement. So make your nest cosy and safe in whatever way works for you – do some DIY, sort the spare room or the attic, organise your cutlery drawer, redecorate if that feels like something you always wanted to do.

During the Covid-19 pandemic we were all confined to our homes, and I think that many of the lessons of that lockdown are applicable to grief. Not least of these is realising that we have to somehow learn to tolerate uncertainty. For many months we had no idea if we were to be allowed out of our houses, what we were allowed to buy and do, any idea how long it would last, nor how the world would look at the end of it. Grief can have that same destabilising effect. Lockdown meant not planning ahead, just as bereavement can make planning ahead impossible. All we can do is take control of our responses. We can't make it go away, we don't know how long it will be here, but we CAN alter how we respond to that uncertainty.

SO TODAY'S SUGGESTION IS:

Draw up a schedule

Be Creative

This one is tough because you may have never felt less creative, and that is completely fine; come back to this another day if so. That state may last a very long time. But you may find, as I did eventually, that grief can be a crucible for creativity. If you have difficulty expressing your grief in words or in any coherent way, then you may find that other means of expression are more suited to getting your 'stuff' out there. For me it is writing, but for you it may be through making art, or music, crafts, cooking or gardening. As with the journaling, please don't think that what you produce has to be any 'good'. The end result is, in many ways, irrelevant. It is in the doing that the processing happens, and no one else need ever see what you have done.

So why do it?
Neuroscience has indicated that the two hemispheres of our brain act differently and have different functions. The left brain is thought to be the rational, academic, analytical side governing logic and mathematics while the right seems more intuitive, non-verbal, and better at processing emotion. It appears, therefore, that imagination and creativity emerge from the right brain.

Each half appears to provide us with a qualitatively different way of understanding, perceiving and storing knowledge and so facilitates different ways of thinking. It's even been suggested that the two hemispheres store memories differently, the left holding the factual memory, the right the sensations of sounds, touch and smell and all the emotions associated with them. We tend to remember how someone made us feel, as opposed to the things they said. This can feel more innately 'truthful' than the facts and can be relevant to bereavement when often we still very much feel the presence of our loved one despite the 'fact' they are not actually present.

We need and use both hemispheres, but some of us reside more naturally in one or the other. During grief, when logic and rationality are not always our friends, I think there are benefits to be had from engaging in a bit more 'right brain' activity. On pages 56–57, if you are interested, there is a bit more explanation as to why this might be so.

If you don't consider yourself a creative person then allow others to gently guide you towards it by doing something non-verbal and looking at or listening to how others have used their own grief as a crucible for creativity. Bereaved musicians have poured their grief into extraordinary musical creations such as the albums *Skeleton Tree* and *Ghosteen* by Nick Cave, both released after the death of his son, while the Mercury Prize-winning album *Process* was Sampha's way of dealing with his mother's death. Visual artist Tracey Emin created several striking works as a way of processing the loss she felt after the death of her mother. Actor and director Ricky Gervais made a sitcom, *After Life*, after the death of his father, and just look at how films such as *Ghost* or *Truly, Madly, Deeply* use the medium of visual storytelling to explore how the search for continued connection can summon up very real depictions of our dead loved ones. In every art form can be found the beautiful results of others finding expression for their grief via creative means. Studies show that 60 per cent of human communication is non-verbal. Whatever art form appeals to you – painting, music, sculpture, design, films, poetry, it doesn't matter which – see if you can activate your right brain and enjoy what emerges.

Engage the right brain

Get out crayons, oil paints, playdough, your old guitar, cookery books, a sewing machine, put on some music... do something creative. However young or silly this might make you feel, hang on to the idea that it can be a really useful way to help you process your grief. So try to enjoy rather than judge either yourself, or the results of your creative efforts. This is about doing, not about achieving.

Emotion and creativity in the two brains

It appears that the two halves of the brain process information differently. The left hemisphere specialises in well-established patterns of behaviour and thrives under ordinary and familiar circumstances. The right hemisphere, on the other hand, specialises in processing new and unfamiliar information, particularly when emotions are aroused – both of which are the case during grief. Based on its specialism each hemisphere creates its own coherent story of what is going on in the world. Its own version feels true for each hemisphere but may be incompatible with the contradictory priorities and values of the other half. Hence why confusion can so often reign.

The right brain is thought to be home to our more implicit, unconscious self. So by encouraging more of a free rein we may allow ourselves to open up to our unconscious more and give expression to what is felt but can't be rationalised. You can think of your conscious mind being like a high-beamed torch guiding you along a rational path, and your unconscious mind having a broader sweep, reaching deeper into the more shadowy nooks and crannies. Creativity can be like taking a broom and sweeping half-formed thoughts out of those nooks and crannies to see what treasures emerge.

Right brain processes are thought to be more adaptive, so by accessing its skills we can better process change, specifically emotional change.

The right brain is more intimately connected to the body and the autonomic nervous system. It is better at processing emotion, particularly negative emotion, unconscious danger and implicit memories.

It is also better at relational communication – so if you want people to understand you better, try to work from this place. I certainly found that when I described my grief in terms of imagery, when I let my unconscious brain go for a bit of a wander into paintings or music or nature, then visualisations would pop up unbidden. By following these slightly cloudy, half-formed metaphors I came up with ways of conveying to people what my grief was doing to me or how I was experiencing it better than if I just described it head-on.

Yet another conclusion emerging from neuroscientific studies is that the right brain seems to be involved in solidifying our sense of self, which can be very shaken by bereavement. Accessing this hemisphere may help solidify your fragmented sense of who you are.

To Distract or Not to Distract?

There are going to be days when you give in to the overwhelming emotions, and other days when you take refuge in denial and want to distract, distract, distract – whatever helps in avoiding anything to do with your grief. Sometimes it will be in your conscious control as to which kind of a day it is going to be, sometimes your unconscious will make that decision for you and you just have to go with it. We all oscillate. And it is necessary to oscillate; we need to swing to and fro to get some respite from the pain, or it gets too much.

Many of you will have no choice – you have to get back to work, look after your children, rearrange your living situation or support a surviving parent. You may find you have to 'shelve' your grief until you can fit it in among all the essential things you can't avoid doing. Sometimes, though, we keep ourselves busy even when it is not strictly necessary to do so, because it can just sometimes be easier to distract from rather than engage with and be present for the grief.

In these cases, how do you know when to give in and go with the distraction option, and when to challenge that tendency? Maybe you never find yourself asking that question, which is great. But maybe it is playing on your mind and you suspect you are doing a bit too much avoidance and need to be in the present moment more. Or you may not be allowing yourself enough distraction and never give yourself a moment of forgetting.

There is no formula as to how much is too much – in either direction. But the imbalance may start to feel uncomfortable to you. You may be worried that you seem a bit 'trapped' more in one state or the other and no longer feel comfortable. Other sections will give you some ideas as to how avoid the immersion occasionally if that is where you would like to challenge yourself. If you fall more into the overly distracted camp, however, then read on.

The temptation to run from pain is of course natural and understandable. When we take refuge in alcohol or chocolate, gambling or partying, we can generally see that it's not the greatest of responses. It's harder to see the so-called 'acceptable' activities of overwork or manic exercising or pouring your energy into looking after others as distraction activities too, but they really are just other ways of avoiding your pain and fear and also need to be examined. Buddhist teacher Tara Brach once said that busyness is the worst form of laziness. And it doesn't help that friends and society tend to be so quick to congratulate you on such a trait; it makes it easy not to have to ask yourself if you are just using your productivity or concern for others as a defence against feeling.

Unfortunately, what often happens is that the distraction activity you have run to – wine, food, work, looking after someone else – can itself become a worse problem than the problem it was designed to distract you from in the first place. It may become an addiction, or it might be that it just stops soothing you in the way it once did and instead becomes a cause for concern in itself. It may be the thing that turns around to bite you when you realise that it doesn't give back in quite the same way that you gave yourself to it. The chocolate that gave you a quick serotonin hit ended up making you fat and filled you with self-loathing; the wine that was meant to dull the edges instead brought up anger and shame and a hangover, all of which made you feel worse than you did before you started on it; and all those people you cared for and into whom you poured your own need for connection and care, well, they got better and moved on and you were left feeling more alone than before – or they weren't grateful enough and you are left feeling resentful, taken advantage of and underappreciated.

On top of the diminishing return of the reward, there is the problem that dissociating or using distraction activities requires energy. Why not instead divert that energy into dealing with the actual pain so that you are not always running from it?

As I said, sometimes it is just what we need to do, but it is good to also know that there is another way. Is it possible – and it may not be right now – to use that instinct towards distraction not as a moment to flee from the fear, but to be present with it? Can you instead be curious about it, get to know it a little better? Approach with caution, yes, as you would any strange creature you don't know and which may hurt you, but nevertheless sit near it, ask it questions, get to understand what it likes, dislikes, needs, wants. This frightening stranger may even, one day, become a useful friend with important messages to impart.

See the meditation suggestions in the Spirit section for more about getting to know those fearful feelings gently and safely.

When you can, try to limit unhealthy avoidance and instead find something that can bring you more into the present moment.

SO TODAY'S SUGGESTION IS:

Get a feel for when distraction is helping, and when it is hindering

Honour Subsidiary Losses

Losing a loved one is only part of the story. You lose an awful lot of other things alongside them as well, and those other losses also need to be grieved and given space and attention. Sometimes it's not always apparent what they are, so start by identifying and naming them. This might help you to start untangling some of that huge knot of confusion and pain you are feeling. It is often in the mounting cumulation of all the smaller, subsidiary losses that come clamouring in the wake of the main loss that we feel adrift and rudderless.

Obviously, everyone's list will be different and dependent on the closeness of who has died, and how entwined your lives were, but I can give you a sense of some of mine.

With Bill's death I lost my husband, best friend, confidant, room-mate and soulmate in one fell swoop. I also lost some, most, or all of the following: my lifestyle, my certainty, my sense of security and stability, my job and therefore my livelihood and my financial security, my future as we'd planned it, my routines, my sense of self, my purpose in life, the will and the energy to exercise and thus also my figure and a recognisable reflection in the mirror. I also lost that easiness and casualness that comes with being with a long-term partner – the ability to be grumpy and completely myself and just grunt as opposed to talk when necessary.

I realised I had to acknowledge all these things that I'd lost alongside having lost Bill – however tiny or seemingly insignificant they may be – in order to fully grieve.

Such an inventory can leave you with a pretty bleak list of

losses, which will of course provoke yet more tears and despair. Yet it's really important to do. Unacknowledged grief will fester and come back to bite you at a later date. Far better to recognise just how much has gone, and properly mourn even the things that may seem trivial in the overall scheme of things.

So how do you go about mourning the smaller things?

- Identify and name the losses.

- Create space and time to feel the pain of them – this might be via walks or meditation or journaling.

- Name the feelings that come up for you around each loss – it might be a physical sensation like a sick feeling in your stomach or a pain in your neck, or it might be an emotion like sadness or anger.

- Have compassion for that pain – give in to it and be kind: allow yourself to say yes, this hurts, this is scary, this feels unbearable and unfair. Because it is. So let yourself stamp your foot, howl, scream, shout and feel sorry for yourself that you are having to do the washing-up again, even if it seems silly to miss the person's contribution to the housework – these things matter, they represent all the ways in which we are now alone and they need to be named, acknowledged and cried over.

- Give the feeling respect. Do not underestimate or minimise the pain these smaller losses can cause. They do not feel trivial in the moment, and certainly not when stacked up on top of all the others coming thick and fast on a daily, sometimes hourly, basis.

It may seem counterintuitive to do all this, but only by giving expression to all the losses, compassionately allowing the pain, will the pain eventually lessen. Only by identifying and giving space to all – the big and small, the concrete and abstract – can the sadness, anger, fear and more rise to the surface, where they can be dealt with.

We don't have to talk about this now, but in the wake of this clearing-out will come space for other things to flourish. In the Spirit section there is material on searching out the new shoots of hope that will eventually sprout out of the nourishment that this compost heap of misery you are currently experiencing is providing. Every action has an equal or greater reaction – the deeper you go in your grief, the higher you can rise as you start to emerge.

There might also be subsidiary losses that could have very serious consequences. The death may have affected how you do your job, or whether you can continue to do your job, which could have financial implications. Your circumstances may mean that the death has put you at risk of losing your home. If you were the carer of the person who has died, their death may mean you lose all the benefits on which you relied, and if you had an adapted car or home then they too may have to be relinquished. You may therefore have serious money worries as a result.

Within the very real need to sort out such major life changes, your emotional needs may get pushed one side. If at all possible, try to spend at least some of every day attending to more than just the practical.

Honour Past Losses

Grief can be cumulative. If you have already experienced other major losses in your life, these will affect how you are managing your grief right now. Sometimes grief that you thought was safely in your past can re-emerge with extra force with this latest death.

Sometimes you will understand that this is what is happening, but not always. Try not to dismiss this by telling yourself 'but that was ages ago, it can't be a factor'. It can and it often is.

You may need to mourn previous losses alongside what is happening right now.

SO TODAY'S SUGGESTION IS:

Allow Space

Allow space to feel all the feelings, for all those who have died, not only the most immediate person.

Allow space for self-compassion around the fact that your responses now may be being governed by feelings and behaviours from the past, further complicating current reactions.

Don't Compare

I hear many people say that they shouldn't really complain, that it's not so bad really, that others feel it worse, or have lost worse. But please, please remember this: suffering is not a competition. The biggest loss is always your own loss, and it hurts. It is completely irrelevant what others may or may not be going through. If you have lost someone, then you are in pain and that pain needs tender attention. It doesn't need to be told that it is less important than anyone else's. The more you push it underground, the more likely it is that it will re-emerge more strongly later.

I know this can feel unnatural. We are all so trained out of what we tend to label 'wallowing' or 'self-indulgence'. We are always told to think of others first. But it is important to give your grief the space and care it needs. Ironically, by focusing on your own pain you may even increase your compassion for others, not detract from it. By practising the tools of gentleness on yourself and accepting how awful you feel, you are more likely to have empathy for how others feel when they bring their own pain to you. You've been there, so you understand them. And you've experienced how tenderness feels, so you know how to offer it to others.

The second way in which I would urge you not to compare yourself to others is in your responses to your grief. There are similarities, but grief is individual and if you don't feel it in the ways you believe others have, or if you think that they are 'coping' better or moving through it quicker, or that you are not feeling enough, or indeed anything, then you are again blocking your own journey from unfolding as it needs to do. There are no rules about this, no absolutes and no deadlines. Do it your way and be okay with that.

Don't Make Big Decisions

Don't get a tattoo or dye your hair that outrageous colour. Don't sell the house, leave your job, start a new relationship. Just don't. Please. Unless of course you absolutely have to; that's different. But if we are talking about the spontaneous, whimsical fancies that strike us out of nowhere, and seem such a good idea in the moment, then perhaps just sit them out. Wait a few months at the very least, until you are a little bit more used to the tumultuous feelings flying around and you can make more sensible long-term choices of the kind that you may have to live with for a very long time afterwards.

The impetuousness will calm down or will at least become infrequent enough that you have longer reflection times in between. Please use those reflective times to decide on the tattoo or the yacht. And then if you still want to go for it, then please be my guest – knock yourself out. Sometimes you really do have to take John Lennon's advice and do 'whatever gets you through the night'.

Out Beyond Ideas

Out beyond ideas of wrongdoing and rightdoing,
there is a field. I'll meet you there.

When the soul lies down in that grass,
the world is too full to talk about,
Ideas, language, even the phrase each other
doesn't make any sense.

RUMI

Body

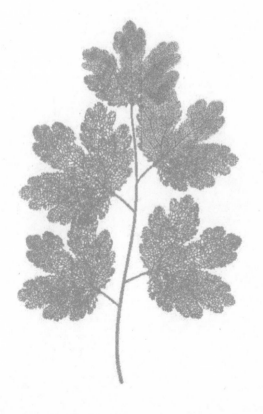

Our own physical body possesses a wisdom which we who inhabit the body lack.

HENRY MILLER

Grief takes a massive physical toll on the body – bone-tiredness, insomnia, aching, appetite changes, weight gain or loss, even physical illnesses and lowered immunity (see page 74 for a list of other common symptoms).

Most of us have experienced how emotional upheaval can be manifested in physical ways – throwing up with fear before a big performance, feeling your knees buckle and needing to sit down on hearing bad news, or getting a headache from stress, to name just a few. It's called somatisation, from the Greek word for body – *soma* – and means that psychological concerns get translated by the body into a physical response. This is not to say they are any less real than other physical responses; they are absolutely real, it's just that they have been triggered neurologically.

This happens often in bereavement, due to the overwhelmingly deep and painful feelings provoked by grief, coupled with how hard it is to express these feelings in more verbal ways. Just saying 'I feel devastated and as though my life is over and I can't think straight' does not come close to expressing what such utter devastation actually feels like, so the body does it for us, showing how much we are carrying via backache, how overwhelmed we feel via fatigue, how difficult it is to process via a headache, how wobbly we feel via dizziness, and so on. And those symptoms are

71

just as painful and just as uncontrollable as any caused by a more overtly physical cause such as a virus, organ failure or a bulging spinal disc.

Some of us don't even consciously register just how badly we have been affected by our loss. Our brains are quite good at denial and our inner critics are even better at telling us that we need to 'just get on with it'. But our bodies don't lie; they are all too aware of how huge this event has been. They will continue to send out alarm signals however much our brains try to ignore them. Those alarm cries unleash stress hormones, which will keep on barrelling their distress message around the body, telling the muscles and organs to prime themselves and be ready for anything. And they often remain in this state of readiness till exhaustion sets in and we find ourselves felled by any number of illnesses.

Two books, well known in the psychotherapy world, say it all with their to-the-point titles: *The Body Keeps the Score* by Bessel van der Kolk and *The Body Remembers* by Babette Rothschild. Our poor bodies do indeed both remember and work as the scorecard for the sad tally of both our conscious and unconscious pain.

If the death has been sudden or unexpected, then we respond even more dramatically. It can feel like our very survival is at stake, and our bodies act accordingly, initiating the trauma response of 'fight flight freeze'. The stress hormones that flood our bodies in these moments of trauma set off a whole cascade of other responses, causing our muscles to clench, our hearts to beat faster, our respiratory systems to go into overdrive, our organs to react, and so on. These physiological responses can sometimes become chronic and cause long-term issues. Another internal system affected is our autonomic nervous system, which regulates our energy and so much more. It is very closely connected to our emotions, in a bi-directional loop, so when the nervous system is out of balance our emotions are harder to regulate and vice versa.

On the plus side, however, what all of this adds up to is that in addressing our physical health we will in fact be simultaneously addressing our emotional health. And caring for our emotional health will naturally also mean taking better care of our physical health. It can be win-win – if we can learn to pay attention to the messages from our bodies.

Here are just some of the symptoms of grief
that can affect the body:

Bone-tiredness Insomnia

Tightness in the chest

Upset tummy

Lethargy and heaviness

Reluctance to move Aches and pains

Lowered immune system

Changes in appetite Changes to digestion

Falling asleep more Needing afternoon naps

Weight gain or loss

More prone to infections and viruses

Physical illnesses

Weakness Discomfort

Dizziness Constipation Diarrhoea

Breathing difficulties

Changes in libido Euphoria

Fight/flight response activated

Move

Research in many different fields shows how moving your body can create a corresponding shift in your emotional state. Movement can also make your body contradict the messages coming from the brain that tell you all is hopeless and that you are disempowered, so it's worth listening to.

Before Bill died, I was very active. I did yoga, cycling, running, went to the gym, walked, all several times a week. I very much defined myself as an active person and I loved it. But after he died my body felt like a lead weight that I was condemned to drag around. Getting myself up and down from a chair felt like a monumental effort.

Knowing how important movement is, I did eventually force myself out for short, slow walks, and a yoga teacher friend helped me do some very gentle stretches, but it took a long, long time to regain the freedom of movement I had once had. My body had shut down and was very resistant to any form of opening up. Just stop for a moment and think about how symbolic that is, how closely my physical state affected my emotional state. Even when I did start to move again, I found I yearned for different things. Bill and I used to go running together, so a combination of my weakened state, and the emotional memories that running brought up for me, meant that I had no desire to restart this practice. Instead I took up swimming, which I'd never been very keen on beforehand. But something about the novelty and unfamiliarity of it felt right and appropriate for the new and different life I was carving out for myself. And the fact that it is a very gentle and quite sensual experience also helped, I think. Just feeling the new sensation of water on my body helped shake me out of some of the numbness and absence of the sensory stimulation necessary to reawaken the body from its frozen grief state.

My local pool has a steam room attached, so I would bribe myself into thinking that if, by the time I'd arrived there, I really didn't feel up to swimming then I would just go in the steam room instead. Then, often, once I'd got my swimsuit on – which sometimes felt like the hardest part of the whole exercise, the getting out of the house and getting changed element – it felt almost silly not to get in to do at least one lap. Which often turned into two or three laps or even more. And I always had the reward of the steam room to look forward to, not to mention the glow of self-satisfaction that came with having done it.

Your own tentative steps towards movement don't have to be huge, and they certainly don't have to be massively energetic, but maybe think about what could be manageable. And I want to stress that the most important thing is doing something that feels right for you and will help you start to move in any way at all. Forcing yourself to do something because someone else tells you that you should is counterproductive and goes against the much-needed practice of self-compassion.

If at all possible, get outside and go for a walk, even if it's just round the block. If you can make it as far as somewhere natural – a park or a wood or some open fields – then even better, as you will then get the double whammy of a dose of greenery and fresh air on top (see the Spirit section for more about nature). But for today just incorporating some movement is your main aim, and walking is often a good place to start.

If you don't like walking, or want to be a little bit more energetic, then of course there are myriad things you can do instead – netball, martial arts, tennis, whatever you like – but no matter what you choose, try to be gentle about it. If you love high-impact sports, or fast-paced things like running or cycling, then great, do those, but try to be gentle in your approach – you are not trying to beat any personal bests here, you are just trying to reawaken your body, to reconnect with it, and trying to dispel some of those stress hormones and the muscular clenching with which the trauma of your grief has saddled you. So, if you find you are running or cycling at a fraction of your old pace, or can travel only a fraction of the old distances, then understand that it will take time to rebuild. Your body has undergone one hell of a battering and may well not feel like itself, or perform like its old self used to, for a long time to come.

Two forms of exercise in particular have been subjected to a lot of research and have proved their benefit to those who have been traumatised. Those are cold water swimming and yoga. There is compelling evidence showing that these are both hugely beneficial for grievers. If either of them appeal to you then it's worth investigating them further.

There are also some therapeutic ways of moving the body, rather than exercising, that are similarly well-researched and may appeal more. Some of these require you to have sessions with a therapist specialising in that modality, some can be done as group classes, some can be done via YouTube or other online platforms. These include TRE; Bioenergetic Therapy; and Somatic Experiencing Therapy.

If you join a group you will have the added benefits of discovering a new community, and if it's something you are learning for the first time – tap dance, ballroom, netball, T'ai chi, fencing or a myriad other possibilities – then you will also be stimulating your brain and encouraging the firing of new neurons. If anger is one of your big issues then any form of boxing or wrestling or martial art may help you channel this feeling into something more productive and so help dissipate it.

SO TODAY'S SUGGESTION IS, QUITE SIMPLY:

Move

Don't Move

There will always be days when it is kinder and more useful not to move.

Given the huge toll that grief is taking on your body, you can and should give yourself permission not to move or do too much sometimes too. You are already carrying a huge weight, and it's okay to acknowledge that. Sometimes it is really helpful to allow yourself to do things more slowly, or not at all. Challenging yourself is great, when you feel up to it, or when the 'not doing' has become too ingrained and is affecting your mental and physical health; but not challenging yourself can be the right thing to do occasionally, particularly if you are someone for whom challenging and pushing yourself is your more usual modus operandi.

So, when the exhaustion levels hit the max do whatever you need to do. Stay in, say no to invitations or duties, stay off work if you can, and don't listen to advice to 'get on with it', whether that advice comes from well-meaning friends or from your own internal critic. You need to rest; your body needs time to recuperate from the onslaught of stress hormones and all that results from them.

You can simply take a siesta, lie on the sofa, read a book, listen to music, watch a film, or whatever 'restful' means to you. Or, and especially if you sometimes find it hard to calm yourself or stop the 'doing', then there are more therapeutic ways, which will actively promote deeper states of relaxation:

Restorative yoga. Forget everything you think you know about yoga – this version is completely passive and consists

79

entirely of putting your body into the most comfortable and supported positions possible (with the aid of blankets and other props), so all the muscles that have been holding and gripping and clenching against the pain can finally let go. You can do this alone with the help of a book or online support, but I would advise going to a class or booking a private teacher who can be skilfully attentive to your needs and lift the burden of having to do it for yourself. Be warned though, the deep release it induces in your muscles can also provoke an intense release of the emotions that the clenching has been holding at bay. So have a box of tissues handy.

- Yoga nidra – this is another ultimately relaxing version of yoga, which similarly involves lying down in a comfortable position and letting go while you listen to a soothing voice guide you through a series of thoughts designed to help both body and mind unwind. There are many recorded sessions to be found online, as well as yoga studios offering classes.

- Meditative body scan – like yoga nidra, this involves listening to a mindfulness teacher taking you on a tour of your own body, inviting each body part to relax in turn.

I would suggest using an eye mask and headphones during any of these relaxation practices, to cut out distractions. You can also light a candle or burn relaxing essential oils or use a room spray or reed diffuser.

Take it easy, rest your body, allow your nervous system to rebalance

Eat/Don't Eat

There has recently been an explosion in research proving the intimate link between what we eat and when, and our mood. Much of this focuses on gut health, the need to repopulate our guts with healthy bacteria to combat the sugar-and-processed-food-heavy diets most of us have grown up with. There are several good books, websites and podcasts explaining more about this and the research is scientifically rigorous. I personally have found that addressing my gut health and being mindful of what I eat has had a massive effect on my mood. Of course nothing takes the sadness away, but at least you are not adding a whole layer of physical downers on top of that authentic emotion.

However, big caveat here – if this all feels like a chore, which of course it will on some days, particularly early on, then I believe it is important, in a different way, to give in to the ice cream/wine/chocolate days. My way of rationalising these days to myself – and I admit it was a phase that lasted quite a long time – was to tell myself, 'a really horrible thing has happened to me, I've been dealt a really poor hand in life, and therefore I am entitled to...' and you can fill in your own blanks here. Mine were chocolate, cocktails and crisps. I also went through a very unhealthy phase involving unchecked retail therapy, but that's another story.

There comes a time, however, when things such as this that you do to cheer yourself up or compensate for all your bad luck become more of a problem than the problem they were designed to replace. Only you will know when that moment comes.

For me it came when I could no longer do up the zip on the last pair of trousers that fitted me, and when I found myself getting out of breath going upstairs. My most reliable 'go-to' comfort activity has always been food. For a while it was great just not giving a damn and telling myself I could eat whatever the hell I wanted. I needed to indulge that part of me. I had no husband, I was at least allowed chocolate! Many, many months passed like this. Until I got to the point where it wasn't cheering me up any more. It was making me unhappy to feel so bloated and so unlike my usual self. It made me slightly sickened and brought about a sense of self-loathing, which really wasn't helping with the grief at all. Quite the opposite. My tipping point had come, and it was time to give my body the much-needed respite it needed from all that sugar. I started to address my gut health, to eat less, and better, and my mood started to lift.

I have another caveat here, though. I say that only you will know when you reach your tipping point, and most of the time that is true. However, we don't always know ourselves quite as well as we think, and if you reach a point where several of your most compassionate and trusted friends are all starting to suggest the same thing – that maybe it's time to shift gear a bit – then you may need to listen to them occasionally too.

Get Some Sleep

It feels a bit monotonous to keep saying 'research shows that...' But it can also be quite comforting, I find, to know that some of the common-sense advice that has always floated around can now be clinically and scientifically proven to be correct. Good sleep really does matter. Without it we are – as with poor gut health – really only adding insult to injury and piling extra problems on top of an already painful situation. Not that we can always help that, of course.

So here goes again – research shows that failing to get a good night's sleep can have debilitating effects on your brain function and on almost every tissue and system in your body. Sleep plays a 'housekeeping' role, allowing rejuvenation and internal spring cleaning to occur.

It's all a bit easier said than done however, and as with the nutrition section, I feel a bit of a fraud writing this because my sleep was disrupted for a long time after Bill died. I can say with sad authority that sleeping is hard. But it is so, so essential, and therefore it's worth persevering and trying every trick in the book. I tried all the suggestions below and, reassuringly, I did eventually start to sleep again.

And thank goodness I did. I can honestly say that the hours I spent lying awake at night, plus the exhaustion I felt every single day as a result, were absolutely the worst grief symptoms I experienced. Tiredness permeated everything I did and meant all the other things I tried to do to help were made just that bit harder. So please do as I say and not as I did and try to prioritise sleep. If the nights continue to be hard then please build in time for an afternoon nap – which research also shows (sorry!) can be hugely beneficial, and which you may find comes a bit more easily.

Here are some ideas to help you address the sleeping issue. I really hope you land on one that works for you.

- A warm bath.

- Aromatherapy – there are sleep sprays for your pillow and oils to apply to your skin, in the bath, or in aromatherapy burners.

- Don't eat or drink stimulants such as caffeine or sugar for the last three hours before you want to go to sleep.

- Don't look at screens for an hour before bed.

- Make your bedroom a sanctuary; make it dark enough, cool enough and quiet enough.

- Get into a sleep routine – go to bed and get up at the same time every day.

- Try CBD oil.

- Wear an eye mask and earbuds.

Other things that might help:
Apps:
Calm
Endel: Focus, Sleep, Relax

Podcasts:
Sleep With Me
Sleep Meditation Podcast

Books:
The Book of Sleep by Nicole Moshfegh
The 4-Week Insomnia Workbook by Sara Dittoe Barrett

Self-regulation and autonomic nervous system

What I mean by self-regulation is our ability to rouse ourselves when low, or calm ourselves when agitated, bringing our nervous system and our emotions back to a more balanced state of equanimity. This enables us to work from a clear-sighted and functioning place rather than an unthinking and reactive state.

That is a very basic summary of what is really a far more complex arena, but I think it's worth acknowledging that our ability to self-regulate is yet another skill that we sometimes lose when grieving. And it's generally a skill that we don't even know we have until we lose it; it's something that we take for granted and which comes naturally in more normal times.

Knowing a tiny bit about what is going on for us physiologically can sometimes help us understand how to regain some control over those unruly mood swings. Or, if it's not at the moment possible to regain control, then understanding why we can't do so allows us to feel less fearful of it.

The autonomic nervous system is central to this notion of self-regulation. Our bodies are made up of many different systems that all work together. Some are under our conscious control, some are not. The unconscious, automatic functions like the cardiovascular, respiratory, digestive, hormonal and immune systems are all orchestrated by the autonomic nervous system. which has two halves that work in tandem:

The sympathetic nervous system dominates when we need some get-up-and-go in our lives – it's what gets us out of bed and out on a run, gets us motivated to do good work, excited about nice things ahead.

The other half is the parasympathetic nervous system, and when that is dominant we can calm down, rest, digest our food, fall asleep easily and basically regroup and recover from whatever the sympathetic nervous system has put us through.

Ideally they balance each other out, and when they don't we can give them an artificial kick-start to make them respond – caffeine, exercise and keeping busy can provoke more sympathetic nervous system activity if tired, while if we are agitated and struggling to stay calm, alcohol, a night in front of Netflix, deep breathing or a massage can help move us more towards parasympathetic nervous system dominance.

In grief, these systems can get completely out of whack and all our usual tricks to force ourselves out of – or into – bed just stop working. The suggestions in this section can help nudge us more to whichever we most need in the moment. However, it is worth noting that the nervous system also works very closely with our emotions and our minds – so by influencing the body in this way we are also affecting how we feel mentally and emotionally, not just physically. On the flipside, by engaging in some of the suggestions from the Mind and Spirit sections you can affect your physiology too. It's very much a bi-directional system.

Ground Your Body

In the early days of my grief I felt as if I was floating. I had a severe sense of disorientation, of not quite knowing which way was up, or how to tether myself. Through no fault of my own, and out of nowhere, life as I knew it had disappeared out from under me and I found myself scrabbling around for a certainty and a way of life that I had once taken for granted.

This is a common reaction, and one way to combat it is to ground yourself. Rediscover the earth beneath your feet, find ways to anchor yourself back down into this life, and re-root yourself into your body. As I say over and over, what you need and how you go about getting it will be unique to you and depends on how you are feeling. But here are some suggestions that may or may not feel appropriate, and may or may not help to ground you, in whatever way makes sense to you.

Garden. This is a very good way to ground yourself, in a very literal form. By getting your body down close to the ground and literally burying your hands into the mud, you cannot fail but be 'brought down to Earth'. There is also something very symbolic about the planting of seeds, which will go on to root themselves but start off as tender, fragile beings that need to be nurtured into life, just as your fragile grieving self must also learn to root and anchor itself again. Just like those seeds, your new emerging self will need tender care so it can grow into the strong, sturdy, well-rooted version of you that you can and will become once more.

If you like the sound of this but don't have your own garden, can you plant a window box? Or join a community scheme or local gardening project; there are plenty about. And if gardening isn't your thing, simply getting out and into nature can also work wonders.

Ignite sensation. Finding ways to reconnect with your body can be done via contact with different textures and sensations. To earth yourself and rediscover your roots, focus on allowing the sole of the foot to find connection with the ground, to be awakened and enlivened via the mindful attention to the feel of the changing textures from rough to smooth, hard to soft and so on. Walk barefoot on different surfaces – carpet, rugs, floorboards or tiles if it's winter, or – possibly rather more pleasurably – on sand, grass, pebbles, or rocks if it's summer.

In reviewing this paragraph, I was interested to see that I had originally spelled 'sole' as 'soul' and I was almost tempted to leave it that way. I think it creates a lovely metaphorical symbolism – letting us know that our soul resides just as much in our connection with the ground, and with matter, as it does in loftier, more ethereal and less earthly areas. It also tells me that you can't have one without the other – how can you reach skywards if not adequately anchored? There will be more on that subject later.

Stand on one leg. To do this, you really have to concentrate. This is best achieved through two actions. First focus your gaze on a fixed point on the horizon – thus reminding yourself that you rely on, and are united with, the world in front of you. A world that, in its immovability and unwaveringness, can steady and stabilise you. Then connect with your feet. Or rather, with the one foot that is in touch with the ground. It is all you have to depend on in this moment, and it cements, anchors, grounds you back to your dependence on gravity, to solidity and the material world made of matter. As touched on above, this grounding allows for an awareness of reverie and access to the loftier world of thought and intellect.

Whenever I feel myself wobbling while balancing on one foot, I use a visualisation to reconnect with the floor. I imagine I am sending roots down into the Earth – small shoots are growing out of the sole (soul?!) of my foot and burrowing down into the ground to find more solidity. I conjure up a picture of a tree in my mind's eye – one of those cross-section depictions that shows both above and below ground level. This cross-section reveals how the roots don't just reach downwards, they reach out width-wise as well, creating a huge skirt with an ever-increasing diameter to anchor me more and more deeply. At the same time, I visualise the four corners of the sole of my foot broadening. I lightly press down into the ball of the big toe and imagine it spreading its surface area; then I do the same with the ball of my little toe, the outside edge of my heel, and inner edge of my heel, creating a broad, level, stable platform to hold me and support me.

SO TODAY'S SUGGESTION IS:

Reclaim your body and find your roots

Nurture Yourself

What can happen in bereavement, especially if there are other family members to be taken care of, is that we go into coping mode. We shut down all thoughts of self-care or self-compassion in the interests of just getting through. But then we come out the other side of the immediate crisis, only to have to deal with the aftermath of the huge toll it has taken on us. We've all experienced working to a deadline and then collapsing, or going on holiday and immediately getting ill – so it can be if we ignore our needs for nurturance during bereavement.

We tend to grit our teeth, power on through, often working without really breathing, our muscles tight and coiled, our cells flooded with cortisol. It doesn't have to be – shouldn't be – like this. Helping others, or returning to work, doesn't mean we need to give up on ourselves. In fact a lot of research is showing two things – firstly that the more we ignore our own self-care, the more limited we are in being able to offer care to others, and secondly that, due to a phenomenon known as 'emotional contagion', it is in fact BY helping ourselves that we best help others. Not looking after ourselves, conversely, can in turn harm others. Seen in that light, does prioritising your own self-care not seem a rather sensible course of action?

Given how important it is to nurture yourself, you may need to put some effort into discovering what that means to you. It will mean different things to different people, but it is important to find whatever it is that allows you to feel properly looked after. We all know the aeroplane safety drill telling us to put our own oxygen mask on first, yet do we ever stop to think about the symbolism of that? Other well-known phrases tell us the same thing – you cannot drive a car with no fuel in the tank, you cannot pour from an empty cup.

And yet for so many of us the notion that we should look after ourselves feels wrong. I hear people use horribly callous words about their own self-care, words like selfish or self-indulgent; or they think if they acknowledge that they need help then they will be seen as weak, not up to it, or simply that they will be letting others down if they let that other, less helpful, mask slip – the 'I'm fine, I can cope' mask.

But how can we continue to give out if we are taking nothing in? All batteries need recharging.

Some people hide behind the need to get back to work because of money, or for distraction. Others need to look after their kids, or their surviving parent, or someone they deem closer to the person who has died, and so throw all their energy into them. I'm not saying those aren't very real necessities, but this just makes it all the more important that your own oxygen supply, your own fuel tank, your own cup of energy remains replenished.

This is equally true if your problem is not work or caretaking but instead a lack of energy, resulting from having sunk into the sofa or bed and done nothing for so many days that inertia has set in and cranking back up to a standing position feels an effort too far. Just doing nothing in and of itself is not self-care or self-nurture; sometimes it needs to be more active.

So how can we start to think about properly nurturing ourselves, finding our own oxygen feed?

Well, bear in mind that self-nurturing doesn't necessarily or only mean doing nothing – if you are someone for whom activity feels more self-soothing and replenishing than rest, then find activities that you want to do, to a level that feels right.

Read a book. Do a jigsaw. Do some gardening or paint the house – or paint a picture. Phone a friend if talking feels replenishing; or stroke your pet. Sing or dance. Really, just do whatever it is that feels nurturing to you and will let you feel fully absorbed in the pleasure of doing it. If it smacks even slightly of being a chore, or something you feel you 'ought' to do, then it is not self-nurture.

Coming up are a few suggestions for things that will nurture the body's senses and at the same time hopefully feel like a treat, a bit of luxury. Add your own ideas to your notebook and commit to doing at least one small thing a day, and at least one larger one once a week. Incidentally, if you can find a way to replenish yourself that also involves reconnecting with the sensations in your body and reawakens your senses, that will have a similar effect to the grounding I talked about earlier.

Awaken the sensation of touch

Get inside clean sheets.

Buy a weighted blanket or a blanket made from a texture you love, like cashmere or felt.

Have a shower or a bath and pay attention to the sensation of hot water on your skin.

Pamper yourself with a facial or face mask, or a visit to the hairdresser.

Go for a sauna, steam or jacuzzi.

Have your nails done – you can of course also do them yourself if that is something you find relaxing and enjoyable.

See a body worker for acupuncture, reiki, cranio-sacral therapy, reflexology or a massage.

Awaken the sensation of smell

Light a scented candle or burn essential oils, or visit an aromatherapist.

Order yourself a bunch of scented flowers; they not only awaken the sense of smell but are of course also beautiful and calming to look at.

Think about other smells you enjoy – put on a fresh pot of coffee, do some baking, breathe in a field of horses or freshly cut grass.

Awaken the sensation of taste

Bake – but, if you have been doing it for the sake of someone else, then do the opposite – refuse to bake! Instead go to your local bakery or coffee shop and order the most delicious-looking cake you can find.

Awaken the sensation of hearing

Listen to music you love through headphones.

Listen to soundscapes such as crashing waves or rain on the roof or birdsong.

Awaken the sensation of seeing

Go to an art gallery and notice which colours or shapes or types of picture you feel particularly drawn to.

Get your paints out, or just do some mediative colouring in, choosing colours to suit your mood, or to consciously try to alter your mood, depending on which approach feels right.

Take photographs. Choose one colour a day as your theme. Be on the lookout for as many things of that colour, natural or otherwise, as you can. At the end of the week make a collage of pictures featuring and inspired by each day's colour.

Meditate on a candle, or a leaf on a tree, paying careful attention to how each gently flows and dances.

Breathe

This one doesn't really have any downsides and is one of the few areas in this book where I am going to get a little bit bossier. My usual mantra, as I hope you know by now, is that you need to tune in and see what feels right for you and you should ignore my suggestions if they don't resonate with where you are at the moment. With breathing, however, I am going to ask you to please, please try to do this as much as possible. I don't mean the unconscious breathing that you do every day and don't think about; obviously you are going to be doing that whether you like it or not. I mean really try, at the very least, to breathe more consciously, and preferably also learn some beneficial breathing techniques. It is important on so many levels.

Gandhi, martial artists, monks, the Russian special forces, athletes, musicians, actors – all these groups of disparate people use breathing to help them focus, calm themselves, and strengthen their bodies, their minds and their spirituality. It's a practice that's been used down the centuries – by doctors, philosophers and religious traditions. It's a physical, mental and spiritual workout.

If you think about it, we can go without food and water for days, but we can't go without breath for more than a minute or so at most. This close connection to our means of survival means that the autonomic nervous system is acutely sensitive to changes in the breath. So, changing our breathing allows us to affect our nervous system, which in turn alters our emotional state. This gives us very real and powerful tools for self-regulation.

This could just as easily have come in the Spirit section – or the Mind section, for that matter – because the benefits of breathing are emotional as well as physical and can calm racing thoughts. That's the beauty of working with the breath – it covers so many bases. On the pages that follow you will find a simple introductory breathing exercise to try, as well as a bit more information as to why it's important, and some suggestions on how to learn more.

Please go very gently, however. If you have never thought consciously about your breathing before, it can be quite triggering. It can bring up a lot of emotion (not a bad thing, but possibly an uncomfortable and emotionally painful thing), so be warned. It can also, in the early attempts, make you feel a little light-headed or anxious. This is just unfamiliarity and will pass, so just take it tiny steps at a time and drop the practice when it feels too much. You don't have to tough it out; you can have another go another time.

One more caveat – if you have asthma or other respiratory issues, be extra-cautious. Stop immediately if you feel short of breath. You may even want to check with your GP before you start, if you have serious concerns.

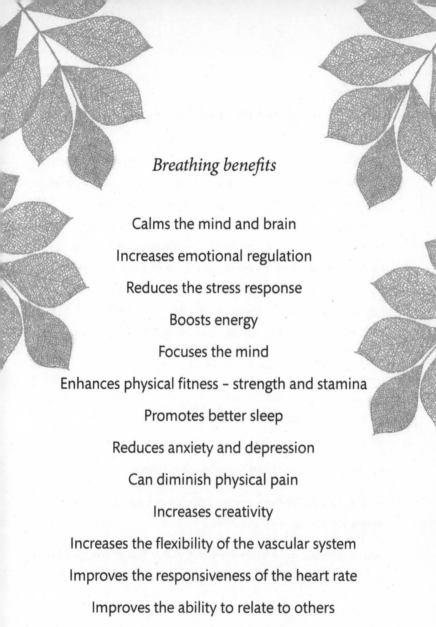

Breathing benefits

Calms the mind and brain

Increases emotional regulation

Reduces the stress response

Boosts energy

Focuses the mind

Enhances physical fitness - strength and stamina

Promotes better sleep

Reduces anxiety and depression

Can diminish physical pain

Increases creativity

Increases the flexibility of the vascular system

Improves the responsiveness of the heart rate

Improves the ability to relate to others

Introductory breathing exercise

When I trained as a yoga teacher I found learning how to teach the breathing exercises that are so integral to yoga to be helpful in all aspects of life. Both on and off the yoga mat, as well as inside and outside my psychotherapeutic consulting room, knowledge of even the simplest of breathing techniques has helped both me and my clients achieve better self-regulation, equanimity and balance. The following exercise serves as a gentle introduction for those of you who may have never consciously thought about your breathing before.

Find a comfortable position in which to sit and where you won't be disturbed.

Tune in to your breath and see if you can identify the start of your inhalation.

Pay attention to the sensation of the inhalation.

Notice how the air feels around the edge of your nostrils as it enters your body.

Notice where in your body you can feel that breath – maybe in the throat, in the chest, in the ribcage, in the back of the body.

It doesn't matter where you feel it, just notice whether you can feel it.

Do any parts of your body move or feel different as the breath reaches them?

If you feel nothing, then notice that too.

Pay attention to the moment when the inhalation morphs into the exhalation. Identify that moment of change.

Notice where in your body you can feel the exhalation.

Notice any changes in your body or in your emotions as you pay attention to the exhalation.

Notice how the breath feels as it leaves the nostrils – does it feel different to how it felt as it entered?

Pay attention to the moment the exhalation ends and the new inhalation begins.

Notice how that feels.

Repeat the above until you are familiar with the practice of paying attention to your breath more consciously, and to the sensations that this provokes.

That may be enough for today, or for this week, or even for this month. Or if you would like to continue, keep reading and expand the exercise as follows.

Start to silently count the length of the inhalation from that moment you have identified when it first enters the nostrils to the moment that the tide turns and it morphs into the exhalation, then count the length of the exhalation.

Become familiar with this natural breath length, just noticing whether they are the same length or whether either one or the other is longer.

If one is shorter, then increase that by one count at a time until the inhalation and the exhalation are the same length.

After some time of feeling each part of the breath being the same length, you may wish to add one more count to the exhalation.

Breathe – with all the same levels of awareness as in the first part of the exercise, and notice what, if anything, might have changed.

When you are familiar with this new pattern, try adding an extra count to the inhalation and spend time seeing if that provokes any changes.

After a few rounds of this, drop the practice of paying attention to your breath and go back to breathing normally. Take time to check in with yourself for some internal feedback – how do you feel now, what did you notice?

In time, when you have become more used to paying attention to your breath, you can introduce other more complex exercises. Below are some suggestions as to how to go about doing so.

- Many yoga, meditation and T'ai chi classes include instruction in breathing exercises as part of the class. Some gyms and yoga studios also offer dedicated breathing classes (often called by its Sanskrit name, 'pranayama', in yoga studios).

- Find an organisation devoted purely to the subject, such as The Transformational Breath Foundation UK, which has many local branches and offers individual, group or online classes.

- Find a website, app, or podcast.

- Buy a book. My own favourites are:
  The Breathing Book by Donna Farhi
  Breathe: Simple Breathing Techniques for a Calmer, Happier Life by Jean Hall
  The Art of Breathing by Danny Penman

Sing or chant

Singing and chanting have both emotional and physical benefits. Physiologically the breath control needed for producing sounds works like the breathing exercises do. The slower, deeper, more controlled and focused breathing encourages a move towards parasympathetic nervous system activation. The increased oxygenation produced aids mental alertness and the energy needed stimulates circulation and muscle tone so it acts as a workout to build stamina and strengthen the respiratory system and its associated muscles – including the heart, which can then function more efficiently. But we are not just talking physical responses – the heart is also stimulated emotionally by singing and chanting, leading to a greater feeling of connection, a sense of joy, freedom and nurturance.

Chanting – the rhythmic repetition of a sound or sounds – is mainly associated with ceremonies either religious or Eastern in origin, and is often included as part of a yoga practice. In some Buddhist traditions sound is considered to be sacred and chanting is used to evoke a sense of connection to the divine.

Sometimes a single sound, or mantra, is repeated. This is thought to vibrate at different energetic levels to which, it is said, different parts of the body respond. Sometimes groups get together to chant strings of mantras in a practice known as kirtan. This involves a 'leader' initiating a type of call-and-response format.

Whether you experience chanting as spiritual, emotionally cleansing or uplifting, or if you simply find it soothing, or discover that you feel better physically for doing it, chanting can feel very healing. It can evoke meditative, peaceful and calming responses. It quietens the mind by fully absorbing you in the moment, providing temporary respite from the sadness – or occasionally even liberating the sadness.

Singing is perhaps more common in Western, non-religious communities and so may make for a more comfortable activity for some, but the benefits are similar. One study has even shown that singing can strengthen the immune system; there were more antibodies in the blood of choir members directly after an hour's singing than before.[1] It's even thought to alleviate insomnia, through strengthening muscles in the throat and palate to lessen snoring and sleep apnoea.

Other studies show that singing releases endorphins – our natural antidepressant – and that it lowers cortisol and thus stress levels.

Possibly one of the most important benefits to the bereaved of either chanting or singing is if they are done as part of a group such as a choir, or a kirtan group. This can promote a sense of belonging and community, as well as perhaps boost your confidence in your ability to be part of something larger, so less lost in your own isolation. For a time, at least. The huge popularity of TV programmes about choirs, such as those presented by Gareth Malone, shows how transformative such a communal experience can be.

And if all this is a new thing for you, then you will also hopefully feel all the general associated benefits of learning another skill.

---

1 'Effects of Choir Singing or Listening on Secretory Immunoglobulin A, Cortisol, and Emotional State', Kreutz, G., Bongard, S., Rohrmann, S. et al., *Journal of Behavioral Medicine* 27, 623–635 (2004).

Yoga

Yoga has been around for millennia. Nowadays people see it mainly as a form of exercise, but it is very much more than that and can have profound effects on the autonomic nervous system and correspondingly on mental health generally. We already knew this anecdotally – there's a reason why it has endured for several thousand years – but we now also know it scientifically. For the last few years academic and medical studies have been able to prove yoga's efficacy in all sorts of areas that can come into play during grief – depression, anxiety, eating disorders, sleep, and a myriad other things we look at in this book. Most specifically, a specialised research centre – the Boston Trauma Centre – has spent a lot of time looking at yoga's effect on trauma; the experience of bereavement, I believe, can very easily be considered to come under that heading.

We've already seen that movement is highly important, so why pick out yoga in particular? Partly it's because the physical activity is not separate from consciousness in the way that more energetic exercise like running or dancing might be – in many ways pure movement can be just another form of denial or dissociation, a way of getting out of your body by just pushing it and punishing it. Yoga on the other hand links rather than separates mind and body – AND works directly on the automatic nervous system, the very place where trauma is embedded.

In grief we can feel dissociated from our own bodies and from the world itself. A gentle yoga practice can help you to reclaim your body, befriend it and develop a relationship with it. Once you start to listen to your body, hopefully compassionately, you realise you have some agency over it. Simultaneously you start to feel more control over those overwhelming feelings you've likely been assailed by. You can start to regain a modicum of empowerment and use your body as a resource, rather than experiencing it as a cause of pain from which you are constantly running. Grief may have made you feel out of control in many ways, so using yoga to focus on the things you can influence, and rediscovering the strength in your body at the same time, can be very healing.

Yoga helps you realise that you have choices about the pain, that you can change the way you feel through different movements, and through changing the intensity of what you do and how you do it. You can monitor and measure how much effort, or conversely how much ease, you need to put in or receive back. Your body's responses will slowly stop being things that just happen to you, that you have no control over, and instead become things that you can influence, that you are in charge of, all of which leads to feelings of empowerment and a greater sense of agency.

Different types of yoga, and different postures, can help influence your nervous system and therefore have powerful effects on how you would like to feel. There are some reading and website suggestions coming up if you would like to know more, and also some descriptions of the sort of postures that you might like to try in order to bring about very different aims – some to energise you and prepare you for facing the world if you are feeling collapsed and sunk into yourself, and some to calm you down, bring you back into contact with yourself, and help you sleep if you are feeling highly agitated, stressed or dissociated from yourself.

How to start with yoga

Going to a class led by an experienced teacher is by far your best option, at least to start with. If you hate the idea of being seen by others and can afford it, then you can always start with a few private lessons till you get more confident. But it's not essential as a good teacher will be able to give you the attention you need, even within a larger group, and should always offer options and variations so you can tailor the class to your own needs.

I really recommend trying a few different local teachers until you find someone whose style you like. Styles and teachers vary enormously, so if you don't like the first class you try, please don't think that is indicative of yoga in general.

Online there are several good ways of finding classes. A YouTube channel called Yoga with Adriene is excellent, and free, and you can choose the sequence that best fits your mood in the moment.

There are also several subscription channels you can sign up to that will give you access to a whole range of different styles and teachers so you can try them all out at your leisure and move on to the next if you don't like them. Yoga Glo and Movement for Modern Life are just two that I know and like.

And of course there is a vast range of books on the subject –
some explaining the philosophy and roots of yoga, some just
offering how-to guides. See what takes your fancy, but a good
starting point for a beginner who is grieving could be *Healing
Yoga: Holistic Healing through Yoga Techniques* by Liz Lark and
Tim Goullet.

If you want some inspiration about how yoga has helped
others to manage their grief and other issues, have a look at a
website and Instagram feed called 'Fierce-Calm: Yoga saved my
life' for inspirational stories.

Yoga for waking up your energy

Any class called dynamic, flow or vinyasa yoga will keep you moving. The momentum from one posture can propel you into the next, not really giving you the time to think about whether you want to keep going or not. In fact, these active versions of yoga don't really give you the opportunity to spend too much time thinking at all. They keep you on your toes – literally most of the time – and that can bring much-needed respite from your thoughts. If you are attempting to stay upright, whether in a tricky balance or just transitioning to the next pose, you have to focus on your connection with the floor and with the world around you, and be closely connected to your body, if you are not to fall over. It's wonderfully symbolic and really can make you forget about your grief, sadness or anger for quite some time.

In terms of specific postures, backbends and chest openers are real energy-givers. It's almost as if they unleash a sort of internal caffeine shot, helping you to rediscover a zest for movement and life. They not only literally open the chest and by implication the heart space outward towards others, but also symbolically you start to feel more extroverted and engaged with a world beyond your own self.

Standing postures help develop strength in the legs and provoke that change of state, or orientation, that can be so useful to counteract the inertia we often feel – an inertia that keeps us under the duvet or pinned to the sofa.

The warrior poses pretty much do what they say on the tin and evoke your inner fighter, the warrior that prepares to face the world and take on the demons.

Incorporate all these elements – they make for a fairly rigorous, dynamic, upright, back-bending practice – and you will have paused the thinking, been absorbed in the moment, allowed your body to release some of its held tension and given yourself a much-needed burst of energy. Afterwards you will feel tired in a different way from before the practice. It will be a physical tiredness that helps you properly relax, so that when you do lie down again – as you should at the end of any yoga practice – your body can absorb and adjust to the shake-up it's been given. It can recalibrate and rediscover a new normal.

Yoga for calming the panic and feeling nurtured

Two yogic approaches are particularly suited to a more calming practice:

Yin yoga is a very slow and nurturing type of practice that will help rebalance an elevated nervous system.

Scaravelli yoga is founded on the notion that we should keep checking in with ourselves, using our own bodies as the best teacher we have and ensuring we never do anything that doesn't feel right. This should really be true of any yoga class, but it can sometimes get lost within the faster-paced ones. Scaravelli, however, puts this principle at the forefront, so you will not be able to forget it.

You can also look for any class advertising itself as gentle or one where you either already know the teacher or can ask them in advance what their emphasis is.

If you are doing a home practice then focus less on the strengthening, energy-inducing standing postures and instead spend more time in sitting and supine poses. If you are very wound up, however, it may be hard to go straight into a calm state and you may need to do some slow, gentle sun salutations or another warm-up sequence that you favour; this will bring your nervous system back down to a level where going deeper into relaxation may become more possible. That way you ease yourself down into it rather than slamming on the brakes.

When this kind of calming and nurturing is needed, take a more static approach and do a slower practice in which you take the time to individuate each posture, mindfully getting into and out of each one and staying there for a while to give you the opportunity to focus and get to know what each part of the body is feeling in the moment.

Stretching and holding particular limbs or parts of limbs, or muscle groups, can help slow everything down and promote concentration.

Forward bends in particular are really excellent at allowing one's focus to draw inward and encouraging your body to soften and release. They promote a withdrawing of the senses back towards the inner self, not outward towards the world, and connect us back to the self.

Have Sex/Don't Have Sex

Loss can provoke an unexpected – and not always welcome – lust for life, which can manifest as an overpowering need for sex. It can conversely make you shut down, unable to even contemplate such a thing ever again. Both are natural, if contradictory, responses to loss.

Wanting sex may be:

- A desire to celebrate life in all its physicality as if to counteract the aura of death, particularly if you have been caring for someone during a long illness.

- A yearning for connection and intimacy if you are feeling isolated and lonely.

- An urge to feel pleasure again in order to counteract all the sadness and lethargy – sex promotes the release of dopamine, which causes sensations of hope, energy and motivation.

- An urge to get away from all feeling – sex can be very absorbing and all-consuming.

- A way to experience a feeling of being in control, empowered and desirable.

Not wanting sex may be:

- Because you are exhausted and drained by the experience of loss.

- Because your body wants to physically distance itself from anything that reminds it that it is still alive when your loved one is dead.

- Because it feels like betrayal, as though you are contemplating an affair, or just plain wrong; if it is a partner who has died, still being in love with and missing that particular person can make the idea of meeting someone else feel far too upsetting.

- Because you feel guilty at experiencing any pleasure.

Both wanting and not wanting sex during grief are common responses. Either may feel comfortable or uncomfortable depending on your circumstances. You will have to navigate your own responses to this. There is nothing wrong with re-embarking on a sex life if that is what you are craving, but as with any distraction activities such as alcohol, or work, or food, try to be mindful of whether this is something you really want and are ready for, or just something to help you avoid your pain for a while. In fact, being mindful and non-judgemental about whatever it is you are feeling – with sex as with everything – is the best way to understand your instincts and feel into what may be right for you. It might be useful to ask yourself this – is what you are potentially embarking on, or alternatively denying yourself, ultimately likely to help or hinder you in being compassionate with your emotions and your loss?

If you do embark on sex with a new partner, be very careful about the fact that you are in a uniquely vulnerable place emotionally and energetically. Allowing a stranger into your bed in such an intimate way could open you up to further hurt. You may get a short-term high, or temporary relief from the reality of grief, but could end up feeling worse in the long run if it doesn't turn out to be what you hoped, or if it results in you just missing the person even more.

On the other hand, if you are holding back from a potentially fulfilling relationship because of guilt then you also need to ask yourself what you are waiting for. There is no clear moment when grief ends; it will always be with you in one form or another, so waiting till you are 'over it' before embarking on sex, or another relationship, might involve waiting for a very long time. If you would like a moment's enjoyment regardless of consequences or the need for it to lead to anything more meaningful, then just go for it and celebrate it.

Ultimately, if you are really mindful and considerate of your motivations, needs and expectations, and if you work to your own timetable, doing whatever feels right for you, then having sex is neither right nor wrong. It just is. We all grieve in our own way.

Spirit

My division of the first two sections of this book into Mind and Body is an attempt to reflect how many of us feel we operate, with these two separate systems each doing their own thing, and with most of us feeling more comfortable in one sphere than in the other. In reality, though, the two are inseparable and influence each other in a series of constant feedback loops. Ultimately neither can really be seen as distinct.

Most, if not all, scientific, medical, therapeutic and sociological study nowadays reflects the acceptance of this unity. For the sake of ease, in trying to reflect this more holistic, comprehensive approach for the rest of the book, I will use a term that has become common within the therapy world – the 'bodymind'.

And yet I've called this section Spirit. Which really can be whatever you take it to be – but I mean it here to refer to anything at all that relates to that certain something bigger than just you, your body or your mind. That certain something that is all about your way of connecting to the world and your place in it.

What does that have to do with the bodymind?

Well, it is just another example of a holistic way of perceiving the world. If our mind and body is working as one, can we also say that it is working in similar harmony (or often disharmony) with something greater? With nature perhaps, or the universe, or a higher power? The planetary system or the natural laws of ebbing and flowing time and tide and moon? Or perhaps it is more to do with a unification with our fellow humans? If coronavirus has shown us anything, it is how interconnected we are with each other: someone coughs in Wuhan, and the UK goes into lockdown. Similarly with the global climate emergency – the Amazon suffers deforestation and people, property and koalas die in Australia, while asthma incidence rises in the UK. There are no borders that can truly keep us apart from the rest of humanity, the animal world and the plant world, such is our intertwining. We breathe each other's air. We hurt another living creature, we hurt ourselves.

Or maybe that's just a little bit too out there for you. Perhaps you prefer to think of spirit as being more about community spirit, about helping and connecting with your neighbours or just your immediate family. That's fine – there's lots of very down-to-earth stuff in this section too, so please don't expect it to all be hippy-dippy ephemera.

Ultimately the notion of spirit means very different things to each of us, and I do not want to be prescriptive about what you may read into, or take from, this section. For some it will mean religious belief, for others philosophical takes on how, why and what we are doing in this life, for yet others it may mean connecting to nature or finding more stillness; some of us may understand it more as a deepening connection to other people – either family and friends, or maybe through charities or voluntary work. It may mean connecting to your own creativity and seeing what emerges despite, as opposed to because of, the conscious brain. Or it may simply be about finding peace and stillness and engaging with your own inner world more deeply.

In a way, to what better use can we put our traumas than to repurpose them for our own awakenings, allowing them to transform us? We can't go back, so we may as well go forward, and we may as well engage with what that future could be. And that may require a more lateral and broadly focused engagement with yourself and the world.

Once again, I am not trying to dictate anything to anyone, but what is extremely common when someone close to you has died is that you start to question the world and your place in it much more. You question where, if anywhere, your loved one may have gone, or the role that fate, free will, destiny or a higher power may or may not have had in taking them in the first place, or in 'looking after' them, or you, now. You may feel the presence of your dead loved one in ways you would not have thought possible before their death. Or you may have had a religion or a belief system that has now been obliterated in your pain or anger at having lost them. That in itself is another loss, which can be traumatic and so cause you to act and think in ways that feel alien and lonely. This only adds to the freefalling, confused way of being with yourself and others.

My first therapist, who I saw when I was in my twenties – in an attempt to slow down my constant activity and need to 'solve' – used to regularly say to me: 'We are human beings, not human doings.' That really stuck with me and maybe that's the un-pin-downable concept I am trying to get to in this section – how and what can you 'be' in the wake of your loss and in relation to your changed world?

All of which adds up to this section being quite broad and wide-ranging. It covers many spheres, including a massively important aspect related to, and indivisible from, the bodymind and from spirit – and that is emotion. Our emotional world could possibly be seen as the element that links everything together. How we feel is so crucial to our sense of self and our sense of others.

In the pages to follow we will look at various things you may be feeling with regards to these less tangible, more transcendent ways of engaging – or not – with yourself and with the world in the wake of your great loss. We will also be looking at other ways of conceptualising and reflecting upon the meaning-making that often comes with grief.

As always, take what you find helpful and ignore the rest.

Some of the
emotional symptoms of grief:

Fear

Confusing contradictions

Anger Sorrow Sadness

Feeling of implosion

Ground disappearing

Tumult

Self-destruction

Numbness

Raw pain Terror Depression

Anxiety

Unsure of yourself

Helpless Out of control

Disbelief Disorientation

Missing Yearning

Questioning

Read Poetry

Genuine poetry can communicate before it is understood
T. S. ELIOT

I find poetry both comforting and spiritually uplifting. I feel it connects me to another level of understanding that taps into something deeper, something that says so much more than the actual words used. It is more than the sum of its parts. The same is true of some visual artworks that viscerally depict my experience. Some music too. I think what I am grasping towards – and my inability to articulate is in a way proving the point for me – is to say that I find that different art forms transport me in a way that defies description. That, for me, is a version of spirituality that has nothing to do with religion or other potentially off-putting notions; it's more a sort of elation that someone or something has 'got' me and illuminated or transported a visceral feeling into something more tangible in ways that I can't.

You may have feelings evoked, elucidated or rendered more complete by an art form. It may be something you will have to discover about yourself. Or you may already know this about art. If so, you may find that in grief this sense of transportation to another realm of feeling is even more intense or necessary.

But back to poetry.

So the darkness shall be the light, and the stillness the dancing.
T. S. ELIOT

Poems connect me with feelings, but so can the manner in which they arrive in my life. For me to sit down with a book of poetry is rare; I am too impatient most of the time. But occasionally a friend will send me a poem that just seems to fit with what I need to hear on that day. The fact that it has been sent by a friend, that it lands on a particular day and often speaks to what I need in the moment, or offers me something that I didn't know I needed, is all part of the 'extra realm' that goes above and beyond what the poem itself (or picture or piece of music – those work too) is saying.

There is a Buddhist saying I like: 'When you are ready to learn the lesson, the teacher will appear.' Some of these poems have been my teachers, pointing me to the next stage of my understanding, just at the point when I need that new door to open.

These are hard concepts to describe, so I will offer a couple of examples of poems that particular friends have sent me, or that I discovered by chance, and which landed on a day when I really needed to hear that particular message.

There are stars whose radiance is visible on Earth though they have long been extinct.
There are people whose brilliance continues to light the world even though they are no longer among the living.
These lights are particularly bright when the night is dark.
They light the way for humankind.

This one, by Hannah Senesh, came on a day during early lockdown when I was feeling particularly alone and particularly distanced from Bill. I'm not sure if it's even a poem in fact, but it reminded me that Bill does still guide me, whether he's here in person or not. He hasn't gone anywhere but has become one with a universe within which we both exist, just in different forms.

The next one, by Averil Stedeford, was sent to me in the very early days after his death and provided a lifeline when I needed it most, letting me know that pain can transform into beauty, and, again, that I can still carry Bill with me in non-material form:

The Heavy Stone

My grief was a heavy stone,
rough and sharp.
Grasping it to pick it up
my hands were cut.

Afraid to let it go,
I carried it.
While I had my grief
you were not lost.

The rain of my tears smoothed it,
and the wind of my rage weathered it
making it round and small.

The cuts of my hands have healed.
Now in my palm it rests,
sometimes almost beautiful,
sometimes almost you.

AVERIL STEDEFORD [1]

First published in *Facing Death, Patients, Families
and Professionals*, 1994 (second edition), then in *The
Long Way Down - Poems of Grief and Hope*, 2017.

Metaphor, Myth, Imagery

Alongside poetry there are other ways of playing with, or broadening out, words and meaning. Things like metaphor, myth and parable speak to me strongly. I am particularly drawn to visualisation, as evidenced by my narrative theme in *Languages of Loss*, which involved a consistent feeling of being tossed and turned in an ocean of grief that had the power to drown me if I didn't learn to lean into and ride its waves. Being aware of the state of that metaphorical ocean on any one day connected me to my feelings in a very microscopic, specific way. Simultaneously it allowed me to see my situation as part of a larger, macroscopic connection to the ever-changing universal pull of nature, the laws of which govern all of us and reveal our insignificance in the wider scheme of things.

Another visualisation that kept popping up for me was that of needing to pick my way barefoot through the bombsite my life had become, slowly rediscovering the shoes and other shields I needed to protect me from its shards and dangers. That metaphor eventually broadened out further to become an image of finding small gems of joy hidden among the rubble.

Another metaphor that I love, because – like the oceanic one – it is grounded in connection with nature, concerns compost. This delightfully alchemical substance starts its journey as unwanted detritus, is thrown out onto a pile of similarly superfluous rot, degenerates further into smelly, rotting slime that repels, before eventually becoming beautifully rich, crumbly black gold from which springs gorgeous, green shoots of new life. The compost feeds and nurtures and provides a wellspring of fertility for the food that will go on to feed us, and the flowers that will go on to delight us.

Compost carries within it potential. And it takes time. It takes as long as it takes, and it is pretty smelly and slimy en route. So is it even true to say – as I do above – that it starts its journey there? Does it really start there or, like the infamous chicken and egg, is it not really possibly ending its journey there – its journey as a nutritious or beautiful plant before becoming compost? The life cycle – our life cycle – really is an unending circle. Life becomes death becomes life becomes death. Billy was a flower who brightened my days and now he is compost enrichening and facilitating my own flowering towards a new version of myself.

Sticking with my nature theme – for a seed to sprout it must break, for a caterpillar to become a butterfly it must transform. Nothing good can birth without a death. And that death is excruciatingly painful. You too can find a new birth into a new you. I know you wish you didn't have to. I know you don't want to. I know you want your old life back. I am not saying it's not utterly awful that you have to go through this process. But you can't not. You cannot have your old life back. Use this rotting compost to allow something new to emerge. What is the alternative? That you stay in the pile of putrefaction and misery? Or that it transforms into the feeding ground for something new? Your sadness will go with you, but it can be transformative even while accompanying you.

You may find that ancient myths of Greek heroes, or gods, fairy tales, parables or Bible stories, speak to you more. Or that it is within music or art that you better find your story reflected. Sometimes a piece of art can just sum it all up. There is a picture that pops into my mind very often. It is an installation artwork that I saw in person many years ago and which stayed with me, coming back to haunt me – happily – after Bill's death. I now google its image often to have another look as I find it so evocative.

Artist Cornelia Parker's installation *Cold Dark Matter: An Exploded View* was created by her having a garden shed blown up, then reassembling it as though mid-explosion. It is an image that sums up the effect Bill's death had on my life – a depiction of fragmentation and materials in a state of flux; an instantaneous moment frozen in time to represent its durational impact; a safe container rendered no longer safe, instead its constituent parts made vulnerable for all to see; an interior become an exterior.

The installation is both solid and transparent – you can look and study each individual piece, and see not only the element but the space around it and also the long shadow it casts in the greater space of the room in which it sits. This is both spooky and beautiful. Each individual, broken, unrecognisable fragment is important and each adds up to a whole that is worth more than the sum of its parts – there but not there. The shed itself is not there, but every part of the shed is there. It is new and surprising. And if I were to win the lottery this is the piece I would buy.

Spirituality

I'm not sure it's up to me to suggest how you go about finding – or losing – a sense of spirituality in the wake of a death. For some of you it will be irrelevant – you had none and seek none now, or you had some before, and still do have some now.

Others among you may find yourself asking questions of yourself and the world that you never did before. These may or may not have taken a religious, political or philosophical form and may be called into question now in either a positive and comforting way, or in a negative and distressing way.

Obviously there are religious leaders from many different religions to whom you can talk about your thoughts if you feel that would be helpful. There are philosophers you may be drawn to whose ways of conceptualising why we are here and where we go next mirror your own. Or whose writings can help you along the way towards finding what your own views might be. Nowadays it's easy to find not just people in your community to help, but books, podcasts, websites, apps, all of which you can dip into and out of and see if anything speaks to you. A transpersonal psychotherapist can also help you explore some of these questions, if you have them.

Your experience will not be mine, but just in case it is of interest, I can tell you briefly my own evolving relationship with spirituality during grief. I am a Quaker and that identity became more important to me after Bill's death. I felt Bill's presence very strongly – still do, although not in quite such an intense way as in the first year after his death – and that convinced me that he is still around – somehow! I also simply couldn't bear to think he had just disappeared without reward for all that he had done while on Earth, so my conviction that he was somewhere blissful in another form deepened. I didn't, don't, try to analyse too deeply what form that might take, or what blissful even means, I just have an instinctive sense that he's more than okay. I also continued to study Buddhism, as I had done prior to his death, and I found much within the Buddhist viewpoints on life and death to be very comforting. In addition, I found C. S. Lewis's memoir about losing his wife and his attempts to understand this within his strong Christian faith to be eye-opening and challenging, in a good way. I also felt more deeply connected to nature and to other people, and on what felt to be a deeper, more spiritual level than before.

My personal experience of feeling strongly that Bill is still very present in my life is borne out by research that shows that this is an incredibly common phenomenon in bereavement, particularly among widows and widowers. Of course it is perfectly possible that my desire to believe he is still around and communicating with me means that I am post-rationalising mere coincidences – making them about him in a way that bears no relation to reality. But in a way, what does it matter if that is so? If believing him still to be with me makes me feel more connected and less sad, then – to me – it is irrelevant what the scientific truth is.

It is up to you to believe whatever you want to believe.

You will find your own way, or no way, of making a broader sense out of your loss.

That may be finding religion, it may be losing your religion. You may feel a presence, you may not.

I don't know if any of this will resonate with you and I can't tell you whether or how to seek your own answers, but I suppose what I can do is posit the question: What are you being opened up to? Willingly or not, you may find yourself questioning yourself and your world. This is not only natural but can be very transformative, so I would encourage you to explore more.

Meditate

The art of listening inwardly for guidance
ERICH SCHIFFMAN

Meditation is a millennia-old practice. Originating within various spiritual traditions, it is now used by everyone from big corporations to athletes, politicians to prisoners, teachers to schoolchildren. The benefits to our bodymind and our emotions are myriad and proven, and it is recommended by NICE (the UK's National Institute for Health and Clinical Excellence) for a huge range of issues. As with yoga and connecting with nature, ancient practices intuitively experienced as beneficial are now proven scientifically to be so. Neuroscientists can see via MRI scans that long-term meditation can actually increase the grey matter in the area of the brain linked to emotional regulation. This means meditators can actively bring about emotional changes by an increased ability to lower activation in the amygdala, the brain's alarm centre.

There are various forms of meditation – the quotation that opens this chapter is but one of many definitions. Nowadays people tend to use the term interchangeably with 'mindfulness'. The two things are connected and depending on who you learn with there may appear to be very little difference, and the distinctions may seem subtle. Advanced meditators and mindfulness practitioners will be able to elucidate those subtleties and differences for you. But in grief, and for those beginning this journey, it really is, as always, more about finding what method and which teacher best suits your particular temperament. There are myriad ways to meditate, and many resources to help you – books to read, classes to attend, apps to follow. Some of these resources are listed here. It may take a while to find what works for you. But please bear in mind a few things:

- Whatever version of meditation or mindfulness you practise, you are unlikely to 'empty your mind' – which can often be what some non-meditators think meditation is all about. It is not. Not discovering an empty mind does not mean 'I'm so bad at this'. How often have I heard people use this as an excuse to give up? Rather, it is about focusing on one thing and noticing how hard it is to remain with that focus. So, every time your mind wanders, the practice is to notice that it has wandered and bring it back to the object of focus – whether that be the breath, a candle, a mantra. It is not about getting cross with yourself and deciding that it is not for you because you cannot immediately stop every thought in your head. If any of us could do that we wouldn't need a meditation practice to start with! It is in the 'noticing and bringing it back' that the meditation happens. Obviously, that is a very simplistic way of describing a fascinating, ancient, lifelong practice of many branches, and I urge you to read/listen to/attend classes with experienced and practised meditation teachers to learn properly, but please don't fall at what you think is the first hurdle.

- Meditation will not always be relaxing or calming in the short term. Sometimes it can bring up uncomfortable thoughts that we would rather not dwell upon. This is painful but can be necessary and can show us all too clearly what we have been avoiding, and why. Over time, there will be an evolution in the quality of the pain if you can sit with it, dialogue with it, and be attentive to it. That way it can tell its story, be heard, be loved and eventually be soothed.

When grieving, the helpfulness or otherwise of formal sitting meditation may vary. I used to meditate quite regularly before losing Bill. Several times a week I would stop everything and sit and focus on my breathing for about twenty minutes, and that provided a calm, still point in a turning world, which helped me regroup and think more clearly. After Bill died that practice went out the window. I didn't want to be alone with my thoughts, nor provide any more space for all the feelings. They were assailing me on far too regular a basis for me to want to create added room for them. So I turned to different forms.

These other forms of meditation may be easier to approach when grieving. If the formal, sitting still and focusing version is too intense, then you may want to try 'compassion focused' mindfulness. There's increasing scientific evidence for the benefits of practices that help us generate kindness, acceptance, appreciation and other positive emotions. At the times when grief is at its most forceful, following a guided compassion meditation might be a lot more achievable than sitting silently with your thoughts and feelings.

Other meditations – often called body scan meditations – actively direct your awareness to different parts of the body, 'grounding' yourself in physical sensations, or exploring parts of you that are healthy alongside all those that hurts.

- Walking meditation also offers the opportunity to keep your body moving while practising, which may also feel like a more appropriate approach.

- Any of these options may prove wiser activities at times than forcing yourself to 'feel' your rawest emotions. Meditation shouldn't feel like gritting your teeth.

In the Mind section I talk about that swing between distraction from, and immersion in, the feelings. Both are useful but occasionally it can be hard to know when we have got too stuck on one side at the expense of the other. It is then that we have to ask ourselves the question: when is it right to indulge this, and when do I need to challenge myself out of it? Meditation can be really helpful in answering this conundrum. After my initial reluctance meditation has become important to me again now, two years on from Bill's death. It offers me respite and clarity from the maelstrom, enabling a deeper connection with myself, and even with Bill too sometimes. You too may find that it encourages you to get away from the unremitting thoughts, to feel into your pain, see it, allow it, sit with it. And therefore, ultimately, to see also that it passes.

Meditation can bring you:

Clearer focus and clarity

Greater awareness including self-awareness

Better self-regulation

Better decision-making abilities

A greater sense of purpose

A more relaxed, calm state

A sense of being re-energised

Increased capacity for creativity

A reduction in stress, anxiety and depression

Greater peace of mind

Greater compassion for self and others

Better nervous system balance and a reduction
in stress hormones

A more positive mindset

Better memory and ability to problem-solve

Where to start

Below are just a few of the places and people I have found useful on my own meditation journey. You may find some of them also help you to make a start.

Teachers
Mindfulness Based Stress Reduction (Mindfulnessworks.com)
British Association for Mindfulness Based-Approaches
(bamba.org.uk)
www.teaching-meditation.co.uk/Learn-to-Meditate/Find-a-
Meditation-Teacher
www.thebuddhistsociety.org

Books
Mindfulness in Eight Weeks by Michael Chaskalson
*Mindfulness: A Practical Guide to Finding Peace in a Frantic
  World* by Mark Williams
The Unexpected Power of Mindfulness and Meditation by Ed and
  Deb Shapiro
Teach Us to Sit Still by Tim Parks
Peace Is Every Step by Thich Nhat Hanh
Radical Compassion by Tara Brach
Loving Kindness by Sharon Salzberg
When Things Fall Apart by Pema Chödrön

Apps
Insight Timer	Ten Percent Happier
Calm	Unwinding Anxiety
Headspace	Waking Up

Seek Therapy

I'm a psychotherapist so you might say that I would say this, wouldn't I; but I think getting some professional help can be useful. In fact, not all therapists agree that it is necessary, but I personally found it incredibly helpful.

Only you can judge whether you would like to give it a go and if so, when.

In the immediate aftermath of bereavement you may feel you need some support and an empathic listener. Therapy is more than this, but it can also be this, if this is what you need. Seeing a therapist does not mean that your grief is abnormal or has to be 'talked away', but perhaps you cannot stop crying or make sense of anything and just need a safe space in which to wail and vent. It is important to take time to be with your grief, whether that be alone or in the company of a trusted other. If it perhaps feels hard to 'let go' on your own, or if you don't want to upset those around you, then having the opportunity to do this elsewhere can be helpful. It certainly doesn't mean there is anything wrong with you, nor that grief is being pathologised.

You might feel totally averse to the idea. It may feel like the last thing you could possibly engage in when it is all so raw and immediate, and that is understandable too.

Even if you feel it is not right in the immediate aftermath, you may find that if many months or even years have gone by and you are still struggling to find a new normality, or if you are questioning where your life is going, or how you got to where you are now, this may be a more appropriate time to reflect back with some space between you and the actual event of the death. At this time therapy can be more than simply supportive; it may also help you think about some of the other things that the grief has thrown up in its wake.

Many people say that they see no need for therapy because they have friends they can talk to. Or they say they wouldn't know what to talk about. Or they can't imagine talking to a stranger about their most intimate feelings, or that they wouldn't know how to go about finding a therapist or know what sort of therapist to look for. Cost is of course also an issue. These are all valid concerns, and I would like to try to address some of them below.

What can a psychotherapist offer that a friend can't?

Unlike a friend, a psychotherapist is trained to sit with another's pain without trying to solve it. They won't feel uncomfortable with your tears or anger, your silence or verbosity. Or even your inability to articulate your thoughts and feelings – they can perhaps help you to grapple your way towards this.

You do not have to worry that you are frightening them, or boring them, nor do you have to hear clumsy attempts to make you feel better. You do not need to worry what they might be thinking of you, because a therapist does not judge. The therapist will not be struggling with their own grief for the person who has died, they will be independent and objective. They have no fixed ideas or an agenda as to how, or for how long, you can grieve. They will offer the time, space and compassion for you to give in to whichever version of grief you feel like, even if that means voicing some uncomfortable truths that you might not confess to a friend – that you feel relief perhaps, or that you feel nothing at all, or that you feel you are 'getting it wrong'.

Beyond this 'being alongside' role, a therapist can, if desired, work with you to explore some of your own ingrained habits and personality traits that may be either helping or hindering you in fully opening up to, or managing, your grief. Your past patterns of responding to situations, and being responded to, may be influencing your reactions now, and these can be compassionately investigated.

A therapist can allow space to examine all the subsidiary losses to have come in the wake of the death, and work with previous losses that may have been reawakened by the latest one.

A therapist can offer 'psycho-education' – they can explain some of the theoretical underpinnings to grief and help your mind engage with what is going on in a way that makes the feelings clearer, if no less painful. They can normalise and explain the commonalities between what to you may feel very unfamiliar and disorientating new feelings, but which all form part of what is known to be integral to grieving.

If your feelings feel too overwhelming – as though letting them out will be like breaking open the floodgates to a huge unstoppable dam of water that will flood you uncontrollably – then a therapist can help you pace yourself. They can do what we call 'talking about the talking about it' as a way of approaching it almost side-on. They can then guide you gently towards learning how to take control of the outflow, so you can be confident you know how to bring the flood to a stop – your hand on the tap in the dam, so to speak.

A therapist can help you be more present and lessen the need to distract.

What type of psychotherapist should I get?

All the research suggests that what makes therapy successful is not the modality that the therapist trained in, but the depth and authenticity of the relationship between client and therapist. I always suggest clients visit two or three therapists for an introductory session before deciding which to choose because, like any relationship, if the chemistry isn't there it is unlikely to be fully satisfying. Some therapists do not like the idea that the initial assessment session is as much about you assessing them as it is them assessing you, so if you encounter any resistance to this approach then you might want to think about whether this is the sort of person you want to offer all your vulnerabilities up to.

Beyond that, you may also want to think about which approach best suits the type of person you are. In *Languages of Loss* I describe several different therapeutic approaches – body psychotherapy, existential, psychodynamic, transpersonal, attachment – there are many schools of thought. You may have an idea of which speaks to you, or if you don't feel particularly drawn to any one type in particular then look for an integrative therapist who has a broader training and so is less specific about only working within one model. Together you can then start to learn which emphasis is most helpful to you in this moment.

How do I find a therapist or counsellor?

There are several governing bodies for the psychotherapy profession in the UK, on whose pages you will find lists of accredited practitioners. Among these are:

British Association for Counselling and Psychotherapy (bacp.co.uk)
UK Council for Psychotherapy (psychotherapy.org.uk)
British Psychoanalytic Council (bpc.org.uk)
Counselling and Psychotherapy in Scotland (cosca.org.uk)
UK Association for Humanistic Psychology Practitioners (ahpp.org.uk)
National Counselling Society (nationalcounsellingsociety.org)
Human Givens Institute (hgi.org.uk)

These websites have more information about what type of therapy their members provide, along with directories and search functions where you can search via whichever criteria are important to you – modality or geographical proximity, or you can look for someone who specialises in working with grief.

You may also be able to access free therapy via your GP practice itself, although waiting lists tend to be long and generally only six sessions are offered.

The above is not an exhaustive list and most GP practices, if unable to offer their own NHS-funded service, can also provide you with a list of local therapists.

The charity Cruse Bereavement Care has a long history of working voluntarily with the bereaved. You can contact them via their website (cruse.org.uk), which also provides a lot of useful factsheets and other information.

Are there other types of therapeutic help?

Some hospices offer bereavement care – sometimes professional, sometimes simply supportive listening – to the relatives of those they have cared for at the end.

Some people find hypnotherapy useful for working on specific aspects of grief such as insomnia or trying to be more present.

You may find that getting away from the everyday and going on a grief-centred retreat for a few days means you are able to engage more fully with your grief. Being surrounded by others in similar situations may feel more supportive than being with those who know and love you but who perhaps can't understand you in the same way. It can sometimes feel that the world is divided into two tribes – those who know what grief feels like, and those who don't. You may need to be surrounded by your tribe right now, people who 'get it'.

The Good Grief Project run residential retreats for the bereaved, or you may find that another type of retreat, such as those specialising in yoga or meditation, is more what you need – the chance to be present with yourself in a calming and supportive atmosphere.

What if I can't afford it?

Embarking on therapy, or going on a residential retreat, is not cheap. One possible suggestion could be to ask a friend to set up a fund to pay for this for you. People are generally very keen to help out after a death, but often don't know how. Might it be possible to ask them to make a small financial donation towards a fund you could access for this purpose? You wouldn't need to use it immediately, it might take you months or years to feel ready, but at least lack of funding wouldn't be the thing stopping you trying it.

You can access free counselling from Cruse Bereavement Care or from your GP. There are also several low-cost-therapy organisations to be found nationally, often through local therapy training institutes. Or ask Cruse or your GP to advise.

Some employers will pay for their employees to have a few weeks of bereavement support or therapy, so if this applies to you, do check whether your employer offers such a scheme.

Do/Don't Plan for the Future

Worrying does not empty tomorrow of its troubles,
It empties today of its strength.
CORRIE TEN BOOM

For me, looking ahead made my stomach clench. The thought that I would have to get through an entire lifetime without Bill made me howl. So, I took on board the mantra of Alcoholics Anonymous and just took one day at a time.

It was almost as though not knowing what was round the next corner meant a part of my brain could cling to the idea that Bill would be round that corner. But if I peeked and found him not there, if I could see the wide empty desolate landscape ahead, unobstructed, that was just too daunting a prospect and I knew I would give up before I'd even begun. I felt I could get through the next day, or sometimes even the next week, but the thought that I had to get through a whole month, or year – that was too much reality. That felt unmanageable and unbearable in a way that getting through a day, or a week, wasn't. Those I could do. I could do them via small manageable plans. The next meal, the next visit to a friend, the next work deadline, even the next TV show; those felt like little oases to head for. Find something to do tonight, don't worry about tomorrow. Worry about tomorrow tomorrow. It's an approach that does have advantages, especially for someone like me who used to spend her entire life planning. I was forced into living in the moment in a way that no amount of meditation had previously enabled. I had to bring others on board though, had to let them know it was fine for people to ask what I'd done and what I was doing, but it wasn't okay to ask me what I was *going* to do.

You may find that the present-day approach works for you too. But if not, if, perhaps, you find the current moment too unbearable and you find it more comforting to think ahead to a time when the pain won't feel so acute, then go ahead – think about something nice you could do in the future, perhaps something that you wouldn't have done if you still had your loved one with you. On the rare occasions I did feel the need to project forward, I would think about taking up skiing and horse riding, two things that Bill had had no interest in and which I had therefore stopped doing. Of course, returning to activities I had loved in my youth was no proper consolation, I'm not saying that, but I am saying that reclaiming or discovering a new part of yourself that may otherwise have lain dormant can inject a bit of energy and motivation. And we all know how much those two things can be sorely lacking in grief.

One other word of warning. Something that I found would absolutely guarantee to send me plunging down into an abyss of misery was to play the 'what we should be/could be doing now' game. Mapping your wished-for reality onto your current reality is so, so painful because it will never match up and whatever you are doing now, however nice, will be forever tainted. Be sad, of course, miss and yearn for the person, but try not to compare how your life should have been with how it actually is.

Feel the Feelings

It is almost too obvious to say that grief provokes a lot of emotion. But many of us don't really know how to deal with emotion at the best of times, so the very fact that we are more emotional than normal can weird us out, on top of everything else. Add the confusing, contradictory cocktail of things assailing us during grief, and it's no wonder we often resort to suppression, or avoidance, or that we try to 'think our way' out of it all.

As far back as Darwin, researchers have been studying how emotions motivate our lives – how they have been crucial to the very survival of our species because they help us adapt. That is, they help us to respond to situations as they arise. More recently, neuroscientists and neurobiologists have been discovering just how central emotions are to understanding the human condition, to our behaviours and to our sense of self. They reveal what is going on in our bodymind – the integration of our thought processes and our physiological reactions, and how we interpret what is happening to us in the moment.

We cannot just 'think' our way out of feelings. They are real, they exist, and telling ourselves we are wrong to feel a certain way just doesn't work as a strategy; it only makes us feel even worse than we were already by adding guilt, shame and a sense of failure on top of what was there anyway. We need to engage with our emotions, feel into them and name them. By doing so, by paying proper attention to our feelings, we can better understand how we are experiencing our inner world and our attitudes to the world around us.

Just as importantly, our emotions can signal to others what we need from them. It is now known that certain facial expressions – the majority of which are innate and beyond our conscious control – are common to all cultures and show others exactly what we are feeling. Emotions are therefore very useful, in all sorts of ways.

So let's talk about sadness, which is the emotion most commonly expected during grief and which can penetrate your very existence, drenching you in it, sometimes agonisingly intensely. It can feel deeply unpleasant, but it does have a function. A number of functions in fact.

Functions of sadness

- It can help us recalibrate, allowing us to slowly absorb the knowledge that we have lost someone important and that there is a hole in our life that provokes missing and yearning and longing for what we can never have.

- It makes us more detail-oriented, more accurate, more thoughtful, and it even lowers our bias and leads to deeper and more effective reflection. This deeper reflection helps immerse us in memories and thoughts of what our dead loved one meant to us, the pain of which makes us understand and come to terms with what their absence will do to us.

It causes us to go inward and slow down; our pace changes, our external interactions change, and as we pay less attention to the outside world, we get the space to pay more attention to what is happening inside.

Sadness shows on our faces and in our posture. These external signs indicate to others that they need to treat us gently, and can provoke an empathic response that ensures we get the compassion and care we so badly need.

It is clear that these functions of sadness are really useful tools to help us adapt to our loss and our changed circumstances.

Other feelings are less expected, less understandable and – to some people – less acceptable than sadness. But they are just as much a part of the mix, and can bring up all sorts of feelings about the feelings – guilt, shame or just bewilderment.

Anger is a very common response, yet a hard one for others to cope with. While sadness tends to encourage others towards you, anger can push them away. This leads many of us to hide it or suppress it, which is doing ourselves a disservice; it's as natural a response as any other. Try to find ways to let it out safely and know that it is generally more about the situation than it is about another person.

Relief is another big one that can evoke shame but which is just as common and natural. It is often, but not exclusively, present when there has been a long period of illness prior to the death. The release from caretaking duties, from worry, from responsibility, from seeing your loved one in pain, can all bring about a natural feeling of liberation and a zest for life. While understandable and natural, it can be hard for others to see it in this way and instead they may jump to the conclusion that you must be in denial, or that you have 'moved on' already. It can also be confusing if you too view it in this way, which only serves to add guilt to the mix.

Also common, but seemingly at the other end of the feelings spectrum, grief can bring about strange surges almost akin to **euphoria** or elation, which can be very disconcerting and unexpected. It is possible that this is connected to the fight or flight surge of adrenaline that floods us in times of crisis and can make us feel energised, and more alive than ever before.

Fear, depression, anxiety – there really is no limit to the emotions that may visit at any time. While this is easier said than done, try to accept them all as part of the maelstrom of recalibration that has to take place as we find new ways of being in the world and adapting to our losses. Mercifully, one other very important fact to have come out of the neuroscientific research (and something that meditation can help us acknowledge) is that emotions are short-lived – they arise in response to an immediate situation and they do pass. They come back, sometimes with horrible frequency in the early days of grief, but they move and change and morph as we go in and out of them.

Manage Expectations

In a similar vein to forward planning, I do think that it can be useful to manage expectations. Don't expect life to go back to normal. Think about (recent) lockdowns, endlessly expecting the end and hanging out for that to happen just caused endless disappointment when it didn't. Instead try to understand that life will never be quite the same again. That doesn't mean it can't be great and you won't feel happy and light and re-energised again, but it won't be the same life as you knew before.

Try being with where you are currently rather than just waiting for the day to arrive when you feel better. Again, think back to the days of lockdown for some lessons in how to do this. Focusing on the resumption of normal life helped many of us through the early days, but once it became apparent that there was massive uncertainty, a strategy consisting of planning ahead actually made the next stage even harder. We didn't know when it would be over, nor how drastically life would have changed. As uncertainty is one of the hardest of states to manage, we had to learn to try to do the things that made the everyday bearable, just as we need to do in grief.

Something that helped me was to hope for the best but prepare for the worst. I stopped waiting for the magical future day when I would wake up and it would all be all right again, and instead I took the position that I was in it for the long haul. I envisaged my worst-case scenario, doubled it, and mentally prepared myself for that. That way anything less was a bonus and, rather than facing daily disappointment that things hadn't changed, it came as a nice surprise when they did.

So try to manage your expectations, not just about the likely end date of the pain, but also about how much you can get done, and how you are coping while within it. You are going through an exceptional time and dealing with a very stressful situation. So be kind to yourself and understand that things will take longer than normal, and that you will 'lose it' at certain times.

Looked at this way, the pain has purpose. It is not just misery, but is potentially life-affirming, even possibly life-changing. Grief can transform you. Often – usually – for the better, however perverse and impossible that feels right now. The new you will always carry the seeds of the old you, but you will be stronger and have more self-knowledge than ever before and you will see the world through new eyes. And that can be transformative.

Take Them With You

The prevailing therapeutic theory for many years was that in order to 'move on' we needed to grieve enough to be able to then shut the door on our love for the person who has died, to let them go in order to 'free up' energy that we could then transfer to our new lives. Not many people subscribe to this viewpoint any more. Turns out that the theory that we cannot fully live if we don't leave our person behind doesn't actually bear any resemblance to how most of us grieve in practice. A few years ago academic research with a range of bereaved people found that they nearly all said that they felt able to take their loved one with them into their new life. Flouting the old theory, none of those interviewed felt they could sever ties with someone so integral, so loved and so important – and nor did they want to.

Far from this meaning they were unable to engage fully with their future – as posited by the old theory – instead they found their new lives were enriched by feeling their dead loved one was still with them, still guiding them. Crucially, the research found that this ongoing relationship was able to evolve alongside their own newly developing relationship with themselves and their changed world. Such a well-forged, enduring bond can, in fact, adjust to each new life situation, just as it would have done in life.

You too may feel your loved one is still with you. I know I do. I talk to Bill, and I believe he talks back. I sense his presence within me, and I feel he is watching over me, influencing my decisions. Seeking his approval, I allow my inner version of him to guide me, as though we were still a team, and acting as a unit. I have 'become more Bill', taking on some of his characteristics, and believing that he can live on through me, through the choices I make. I have not stopped loving him and I still feel his love for me.

So it is a relief to find that the research suggests that most of us feel this way and that this is healthy. You do not need to leave anyone behind if you don't want to, nor should you feel guilty for adapting to the reality of life as it is now. I know Bill wants me to live my best life and to use his death to do more than I might have been capable of otherwise.

In the early days of my bereavement, I saw a play at the theatre that moved me very much and seemed to articulate some of what I was feeling around how to move forward. *The Inheritance* by Matthew Lopez is a long cry of grief over the AIDS plague of the eighties, and this storyline runs alongside the personal bereavement of a character – Henry Wilcox – mourning his lover, Walter. A theme of building something positive from a person's death emerges. Here that means taking the sacrifices of the AIDS generation as a spur to living a fuller life. In its final lines, Henry asks Walter's ghost what he can do now, to which Walter tells him that he can do what they could not. He can live.

This to me sums up the notion of letting your loved one live on in your inner world, but also in the ways that you live in your outer world. I feel it would be a betrayal of the life Bill wanted me to have if I didn't grab it with both hands and live it to the full, feeling I am doing it for both of us.

This, in a way, has become my mantra since Bill died – I can repay his love and his life, by going on living, by doing the things that he cannot, in a way that he would approve of, and by living my own life to the utmost.

SO TODAY'S SUGGESTION IS:

**Allow your loved one to live on in you
and to guide you into new and exciting adventures**

Quieten the Critic

If you have a moment of happiness, or a moment of forgetting your grief, you may feel guilty. That's part and parcel of this whole process. The guilt doesn't mean that you are a bad person or that you have done anything wrong. You need to ignore the grief sometimes. You cannot live the rest of your life never finding joy again. It doesn't mean you have forgotten your loved one, nor that you didn't love them, or have stopped loving them. But you do not have to die with them. You have to live, and that life has to be worth living. This chapter is about quietening the critical inner voice that tells you otherwise or ticks you off for not remaining stuck in your misery.

It's also for those of you who might have the opposite problem. Perhaps your experience is different in that you can never ignore the grief even for a moment, have never found any moments of happiness. If that is you, then your internal voice may conversely be telling you to 'buck up', 'stop wallowing' and 'get over it'. You too need to quieten that bullying critic.

Whatever it is your critic is saying, it is unhelpful. You do not need this inner bully. Is grief really not hard enough already without constantly being told you are a bad person and are getting it wrong all the time? Do you really need to add that extra layer of cruelty on top of an already pitiless situation? You need to learn to turn the volume down on this nasty inner soundtrack. But how?

🍃 Start by identifying the critical voice and the mantras it likes to throw at you.

158

🍃 Write a list of its favourite and most frequent sayings.
This might be:

Stop being miserable.
Stop being happy
Stop... something else.
Start... something else.
Get over it...
Stop wallowing...
This has gone on long enough...
This hasn't gone on long enough...
You're feeling too much...
You're not feeling enough...
Be different to how you are being...

🍃 Understand that your critic is exceedingly good at what it
does. There are any number of variations that it may choose
to hit you with at any one time. Maybe all of them on a loop.
The critic knows that if you are able to make peace with one
variation of its ticking-off, it can just as easily pick another
and start up on that and you will more than likely believe
that one too.

🍃 Accept that you cannot win against the critic, it's just too
well practised at finding yet another of your buttons to
push and then pressing it relentlessly till you feel utterly
worthless.

🍃 Diminish its power. If you cannot win, then deal with
it less combatively, and reduce its influence. Even if you

cannot drown it out completely, you can quieten it, lower its volume, pay less attention and approach it like the nasty bully it is.

- Imagine that it is doing this to a friend of yours. Imagine speaking to a best friend in this harsh way, or allowing anyone else to do so, and if that idea horrifies you then please show yourself the same consideration, don't listen, and give yourself a break.

- Know that you are doing the best you can in a truly agonising situation. You are getting through in the only way you can. The actual pain is bad enough – there really is no need to pile subsidiary pain on top by telling yourself you shouldn't feel as you do.

- Focus on the things that you can be proud of in order to counteract the negativity coming from the critic. It's been shown that acknowledging small everyday wins can have an exponentially large impact, especially in times of uncertainty. Consistently recognising such incremental wins has been shown to increase people's engagement in their work and their happiness.

THERE IS MORE ABOUT THIS IN THE FOLLOWING
SECTION ON SELF-COMPASSION, SO MY
SUGGESTION TODAY IS A SIMPLE ONE:

Celebrate small achievements

This can be as simple as celebrating that you got dressed today,
that you got yourself out the house, made a meal, booked a
plumber, went a whole hour without crying, planned a nice
outing, laughed at a friend's joke. Doesn't matter what – just
celebrate how you have done something today that you couldn't
do yesterday.

Practise Self-compassion

We can let the circumstances of our lives harden us so that we become increasingly resentful and afraid, or we can let them soften us, and make us kinder. You always have the choice.'
THE DALAI LAMA

Over the last few years research has shown how important practising self-compassion is to our mental and physical health. It can change the way we think, feel and act.

Yet it is all too common for us to dismiss the notion of self-compassion as being too self-indulgent, weak, or soft, or to think that we are undeserving of it. However, as we can see from the nurture section, if we don't put our own oxygen mask on first then we will not survive long enough to put anyone else's on either.

So how do we go about dissolving that innate resistance that so often comes up at the thought?

How about we start with re-conceptualising? By this I mean choosing a different name, if words like 'nurturance' and 'compassion' are too loaded, for you, with connotations of weakness or selfishness. What word might make the notion more palatable to you and allow you to ease up on the self-criticism and see it instead as a necessary part of the grief journey? How can you reframe it in more positive terms, and so eliminate those negative labels from your vocabulary?

For instance, might any of these words or notions work better for you?

Renewal, **rest**, refurbishment, **repair**, restoration, renovation, **restitution**, return, **recreation**, feeding, **maintaining**, optimising, **refuelling the tank**

Or might it be helpful to think of it in terms of caring for your tools?

Opera singers know to rest their voice, carpenters sharpen their axes and chisels, ballet dancers and footballers massage their legs and feet, racing car drivers oil their engines.

If you think of your 'instrument' as being yourself and your compassion, then that too needs just as careful maintenance. Without oxygen, without petrol in the tank, you cannot keep going, nor can you keep on helping others if that is part of your remit. If you can't do it for you, then do it for them. But please also spend some time pondering that – why does doing it for someone else make it more palatable? Are they really so much more deserving than you of a bit of kindness?

Even if you are able to reframe the concept into something that you can intellectually see as a good thing, putting it into practice can be hard. It is a practice that you have to learn, one that requires discipline.

That may feel beyond you right now, and that's fine. But it may also help to know that research shows that regular practising of compassion makes us less self-critical, less anxious and less depressed. It also improves our sense of well-being and satisfaction in our relationships.

On the next page are some practical steps you can take that may help dissolve your resistance to self-nurture.

Take an inventory

🍃 Identify the biggest demands made of you – who, what, when?

🍃 Identify the ways in which you self-care at the moment – how much time do you devote to each element, and how effective is it in providing you with the oxygen of replenishment?

Create a timetable

🍃 Look for small ways in which you can say no to the worst and/or biggest parts of the demands on your time and energy.

🍃 Schedule in time for yourself, to do something you really enjoy and/or find calming.

Create boundaries

🍃 Be disciplined about sticking to the new plan and help others to understand why it is important that you do so.

Do regular self-check-ins

The more familiar you are with 'normal' the quicker you will spot when you are running out of air, and the quicker you can act to remedy it. Spend a quiet few minutes with yourself each day taking an internal weather report. Ask yourself how you feel on physical, mental and emotional levels, and get to know what feels usual, and what feels out of the ordinary. If out of the ordinary, then maybe you need to do something to address that.

Rewire your neurons

Once you settle on the word or notion that works for you and allows you to sign up to this idea, then use it as a mantra to replace the tired old ones like self-indulgence. Stick the word on a Post-it note on your bathroom mirror so it's the last thing you see at night and the first thing you see in the morning. Or on the kettle so you can't avoid it when making a cup of tea.

Connect With the Natural World

Research in all sorts of areas is proving just how beneficial connection with the natural world can be to both physical and mental health. And there are so many different – and simple – ways in which you can do this. You can go for a walk in nature, do some gardening, or get a pet. If you need more help, or someone to guide you, then follow the science and be more targeted about it depending on where your interests lie. For instance:

Forest bathing

In Japan, the practice of forest bathing, *shinrin-yoku*, is promoted at governmental level. It's proven to reduce cortisol, blood pressure and heart rate while promoting the immune system, parasympathetic nervous system, concentration and memory. Reaping the benefits is as easy as walking or sitting in a forest and drinking the trees in through your senses; the smell, sound and sight of them. Or you can sign up for a guided experience at various forests around the UK. In some countries, including Japan and the USA, forest bathing therapists are trained in guiding you through a whole forest bathing ritual.

Gardening

Similarly, the benefits of gardening are well proven – to the point of even being prescribed by certain GPs. It reduces depression and anxiety while boosting mood and self-esteem. Gardening is a wonderfully symbolic way to help remind us of the duality of nurture – we tend to our plants and they in turn tend to us, giving back as much as we have given. It also teaches us about absence and rejuvenation – we have to see our beloved plants die but we also see the continual re-emergence of others, repopulating our inner landscape as they do our outer one, revealing how change, renewal and regrowth is natural and necessary – the cycle of life rendered visible in all its beauty and sadness. *The Well Gardened Mind* by Sue Stuart-Smith is an excellent book chronicling the therapeutic benefits of gardening. To work therapeutically with someone trained in horticultural therapy, try the Horticultural Therapy Trust.

Psychotherapy outdoors

There is no one overarching consensus on how to practise psychotherapy outdoors, but psychotherapists and psychologists from different traditions are researching and experimenting with this as a possibility. Ecotherapy, green therapy and wilderness therapy are relatively new terms for a range of different therapies exploring the theme of working therapeutically with the outdoors in various forms.

Animal-assisted therapy

Animals have been used for therapeutic reasons for thousands of years. They have a lack of artifice, an authenticity, and an uncanny ability to read and respond to human emotions that is hard not to enjoy. And that's before you even get on to the self-evident benefits of companionship, cuddle-ability, and having to care for something (someone?) other than yourself, which can provide a purpose in life, something that often goes missing during severe grief. My two cats have absolutely been my lifeline since Bill died, offering me more than I can articulate. Cats and other pets, often dogs, are regularly and increasingly used in social and mental healthcare settings to improve physical and mental well-being. Equine therapy (also called hippotherapy) is another growing field of research, with horses having shown themselves to be particularly good at fostering change in humans. They are herd animals, so are particularly good at bonding, and are also prey animals, meaning they can very quickly read and mirror body language. They tend to have big personalities with both a fun side and a nurturing side to their characters as well. As with most forms of therapy, a targeted search on one of the approved therapy directory websites will help you find an equine therapist near you if you fancy giving it a go.

Vitamin D

On a physiological level, we now know how crucial vitamin D is for general health, and how the best source of vitamin D is sunlight. Just one more argument for getting outside and feeling the sun on your skin and turning your face to the sky.

Resources for connecting with nature

Books

The Well Gardened Mind by Sue Stuart-Smith
Rewild Yourself by Simon Barnes
H is for Hawk by Helen Macdonald
The Nature Fix by Florence Williams
Into the Forest: How Trees Can Help You Find Health and Happiness by Dr Qing Li
Ecotherapy: Healing with Nature in Mind by Linda Buzzell
Wild Therapy: Undomesticating Inner and Outer Worlds by Nick Totton
Walden by Henry David Thoreau

Websites

For social and therapeutic horticulture:
thrive.org.uk
horticultural-therapy-trust.org

For an ecotherapist or equine therapist:
bacp.co.uk
wildtherapy.org.uk
counselling-directory.org.uk

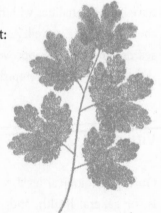

Look For the Gems

The wound is where the light enters
RUMI

A recurring visualisation in the early days of my grief was that my life had exploded, and I was picking my way through the resulting rubble-strewn bombsite. What I came to discover was that there were beautiful gems to be found within that rubble. Some of these I found despite the awfulness, while some came as a result of it – things that I would never have discovered without the explosion revealing them. I call this collateral beauty.

Therapeutically this concept is called post-traumatic growth. We can use our traumas as springboards towards greater depths of self-knowledge, compassion and connectedness. If I look at my own 'gems' – and I admit it took a very long time for them to reveal themselves – I can say that I have discovered the following:

- A greater sense of connection – with others, with myself, with nature, with a higher power.

- Deeper empathy and compassion – for myself and for others.

- A sense of 'aliveness' that came with the realisation of how short life is, and that we really might not get a tomorrow. I felt filled with the desire to get on with living life to the full and not waste the time I have. Part of me wonders if I was

171

sleepwalking through my previous existence, unaware of just how precious and impermanent life really is.

- A stronger faith in humanity and in people's kindness and willingness to step up and put their own needs to one side. And my resulting desire to honour that and to give back.

- A broader definition of family and a realisation of how wonderful my friends are.

- A better relationship with myself. I got to know myself intimately, saw which of my age-old habits were helpful and which were less so. I got to challenge all my established ways of being, thinking and feeling. When circumstances bring you face to face with your deepest fears you start to understand how many defences and distractions you normally hide behind. Then you can start to dismantle them.

- I became hyper-aware and awake to the world around me. I developed a deeper appreciation of having the time to literally stop and smell the flowers more, be 'in the moment' more. This brought me a slower, enjoyable and thoughtful pace with a richer and more concentrated focus.

- A sense of joy in discovering how loved I am, how selfless and giving my friends could be, how humour can be found even in adversity, how creative I can be.

- And most importantly, from the depths of my despair I discovered that I can survive anything, and that nothing can frighten me any more as I have already survived my worst nightmare. All of which gives me greater confidence in my own strength, resilience and adaptability.

You will have to find what your own gems are, and you may not be ready to do that right now, which is fine; it can't be rushed. If when you are ready they don't reveal themselves naturally, then on a more practical level it may be that you can kick-start the process. Here's a suggestion as to how to do that.

A daily gratitude list

🍃 At its most basic, this means taking a few minutes at the start or end of each day to list three things for which you are grateful.

🍃 Or expand this out to a whole journal entry, or a letter to a person to whom you are grateful.

🍃 Research shows that focusing on what we are grateful for every day can have huge mental health benefits, especially in reducing anxiety and depression. It appears that it makes it harder to ruminate on negativity, and Cognitive Behavioural Therapy tells us that where we focus our thoughts, our moods often follow.

Do it regularly
Like many of the suggestions in this book however, it is a practice that needs to be done consistently. Just dipping in and out for a

day or two will have no lasting effects. MRI scans have shown that over time, it can lead to visible changes in the brain, with those who kept a gratitude journal for at least three months showing greater neural sensitivity in the medial prefrontal cortex, the area associated with learning and decision-making.

Be authentic and specific

Don't make it about the things that you feel you *should* be grateful for, but the things that you are genuinely grateful for. You might find yourself saying something like, 'I can't complain because I have a nice house and nice kids and nice friends.' That's not real gratitude, that's shaming yourself for being unhappy when you have 'things'. Of course you have 'things', few of us have absolutely nothing nice in our lives, but you don't have to be grateful for them if they are not providing any consolation right at this moment.

Instead, what are you really authentically grateful for, what has lifted your mood even for a second? The nice piece of chocolate, the feel of the warm bathwater on your skin, the sight of a colourful flower, the uplifting picture you saw on Instagram, the fact that the sun shone, or you went an hour without crying? Be true to what really made today feel worth it.

Don't worry if you can't right now

When the waves of grief are coming thick and fast, this very notion might feel like an impossible dream. This does not mean using it as another stick with which to beat yourself. Always remember how important the self-compassion suggestion is and if you are not in a gratitude headspace right now, then move on to another section more in tune with where you are.

Don't ignore the rubble

I'm also not suggesting that we should only focus on the gems – I am never going to not see the rubble and sadness of life without Bill – but what I can see is that the two things exist alongside each other, that it is, in fact, that very rubble that has revealed their hiding places. I may never have known of their existence without the implosion of life as we knew it, and I choose to believe that it is Bill who has placed those things there for me to find.

Use it as a lifeboat

When faced with catastrophe we can find out who we really are and what we are capable of. We can let that knowledge drown us, or we can use it as a lifeboat to help lift us up and out of the norm and reveal to us that we can rise to this awful challenge we have been set. Can gratitude for what you have left be your lifeboat?

SO TODAY'S SUGGESTION IS:

Start a gratitude journal and see what gems emerge from your rubble

Do something for someone else

A very important gem I found was the joyful mutuality that came from offering help and doing something for someone else.

Once again this is something that it may take you a long time to feel ready for. I initially tried to do this very soon after Bill's death, volunteering with a homeless charity, but I was just not resilient enough to help anyone at that point and ended up more miserable than before. Several months later, however, I tried again in a different role at a refugee charity and found it lifted my mood, elevating me above and out of my own experience.

I found some purpose by turning my focus towards those who needed even more help than I did. Grief can strip us of purpose and meaning, yet they are so necessary to a life worth living. Having a sense of usefulness and a notion – however vague – that we have something to offer, that we have a reason to keep going, can be very healing.

We saw that a similar thing happened spontaneously when lockdown began – disparate communities banded together to find out who among them most needed help and then set about providing that help, sometimes in ingenious ways. For many people this was what got them through those early, frightening days because not only did it show us that we had something to offer, it provided a sense of community and made us feel less alone.

Certainly for me, when I looked for ways to help others I got as much as, if not more than, I gave in terms of gaining deeper and broader connections, new and improved relationships.

I think the benefits of thinking about others could be listed like this:

- You will have created for yourself a community and sense of belonging and being needed.

- You will know you have done something good.

- You will have created purpose and meaning in your life.

- You will have taken time out of your own pain.

- You will have altered your brain chemistry for the better. Any sort of caring activity encourages the release of neurochemicals that satisfy the reward centres in our brain. Oxytocin, the bonding hormone, and the natural opioids such as beta-endorphins are all stimulated by looking after others. If you think about it in evolutionary terms, this makes sense – the survival of the species requires us to care for others, so naturally our physiology would be wired to reward us for doing so with a surge in happy hormones.

Celebrate Joy

There are always flowers for those who want to see them.
MATISSE

Now this may seem like an anomalous section, and perhaps feels impossible to you right now. May even make you angry in fact. I know that in the early days of my grief, when people tried to cheer me up by telling me it would get better and easier, I felt outraged. Why would I want it to? My grief felt – and indeed was – a necessary expression of my devastation, of my love for Bill, of my inability to imagine any sort of life, let alone a life that had any pleasure in it, without him. I didn't want to feel better in any way; to allow for that possibility felt like a betrayal of Bill and our relationship.

And yet moments of joy did come, and continue to come, more abundantly. And with the benefit now of two and half years since losing him, I can see absolutely that those moments do not betray him at all. On the contrary, I feel I am honouring him by carrying on with my life in a way that would make him happy, and which I know is only possible because of him – because he taught me what joy was, what internal self-sufficiency was. He set me up to survive him, and to survive him in the Gloria Gaynor sense of lusting after life and giving it all I've got.

In *Languages of Loss* I wrote of how even in the early days I would – despite myself – occasionally get the giggles at the ludicrousness of some of the interactions I had with people or situations. I would find myself laughing at comedies on the telly, I would enjoy a nice chat with a friend, take pleasure in stroking my cats, appreciate the deliciousness of a nice meal. These episodes took me by surprise given my fury in the face of the well-meant suggestions from others that I might find pleasure ever again. I mused about whether they meant I had retreated into denial and wasn't really engaging with reality. Research, though, told me that this pendulum swing of emotions was completely natural and all part of the process.

As I have continued to read and follow the ever-growing body of academic research into what people report about grief, I can see not only how common this oscillation is, but also how important it is to find joy. The momentary respite it brings is what makes the pain tolerable. Research with bereaved spouses showed that those who laughed and smiled the most had the best long-term mental health. Other studies have proved that people who experience genuine laughter are more perceptive to detail and nuance, have better and more satisfying relationships and are more successful at adapting and adjusting. All of which is to say that joy may feel a long way off right now, but when you do find moments of genuine joy, laughter and happiness please don't feel too guilty. Instead, if you can, make the most of them, safe in the knowledge that you are helping to heal yourself by doing so.

None of the traditional grief theories leave much space or allow for any type of positive emotions. More recent research, however, is proving how common these are, and how important they are for successful adaptation and long-term mental health. Please give free rein to your moments of joy.

Some believe, and I think I do too, that happiness has to be worked at. Frieda Hughes, the daughter of Sylvia Plath and Ted Hughes, has known far more than her fair share of grief. She said, 'Happiness has to be worked at. I believe it has to be earned. It's like a marriage or a friendship, or any kind of relationship.' If joy and happiness feel a long way off, go and seek them, if you can. Call your funniest friends, watch the most hilarious comedies, engage in the most joyful activities you can, and see if you might slowly start to open up to the notion of allowing humour, fun and joy back in to your life.

Everyday

Even though your life may well have imploded in the wake of your loved one's death, unfortunately the everyday annoyances and admin of normal life just keep coming. It can be hard enough keeping on top of the regular things you have to do, let alone taking on board all the extra and unfamiliar tasks that a death throws your way. And of course the arrival of the Covid pandemic and the unprecedented lockdown that resulted has brought a whole raft of other complications in its wake for those bereaved during that time.

There are some very good support groups that can help you through, some of which are better at emotional support, some at the practical. A list of these follows later.

But first, here are some of those extra things that you may have to think about organising.

Letting friends and family know

Personally, I found this torturous. Every new phone call forced me to relive the horror – having to say the words, having the reality hammered home by saying it out loud, having to cope with the reactions of those I was telling.

You may not feel this. You may find comfort in hearing the voices of those who are as shocked and upset as you are. But if not, then delegate. Work out who you need to tell personally, and delegate the telling of everyone else to others. Make sure these people know whether you are ready to receive phone calls and/or visits so that they can relay this information at the same time. Ask them to keep lists as to who they have told and who those people will in turn tell. These lists can also then be useful when you are ready to announce details of the funeral.

With those you do need to tell personally, be careful to pace yourself and have someone close nearby to hold your hand or support you while you do it.

Today of course we have the whole social-media world to cope with as well, and that can get a bit out of control, so you will need to think about if and how you use it. You may prefer to make an announcement this way rather than in person, or you may need to appoint someone to monitor the accounts for you.

The social media accounts of the dead person can sometimes be changed to memorial pages, and you can decide whether to let people leave messages on there or not.

Registering the death

You need to get a certificate from the hospital where the death occurred, and you need to take this to your local Town Hall Register Office to register the death. There you will be issued with a death certificate. Always ask for at least ten copies because you will repeatedly be asked to send proof of death to all sorts of organisations as you try to close down accounts – as we will see. You will often also be asked to provide other documentation, such as your marriage certificate for a spouse's death, and sometimes even a birth certificate or passport. Always include an SAE for anything you send out. Dispatch a friend to get envelopes and stamps.

Letting official bodies know

The number of ways in which we are connected to, and do business with, people and systems is huge.

Below is just a selection of some of the organisations you will need to inform, and things you will have to think about:

Finances

Banks How many/which bank accounts were there and how many in single or joint names? These need to be shut down or transferred and you will need multiple copies of the death certificate and probate forms in order to do this. You will need to transfer all the direct debits and standing orders going out, as well as inform anyone who regularly pays in.

Credit cards How many/which credit cards were there that need to be paid off and shut down?

Debts Are there any other outstanding debts that need to be settled?

Savings and investments Were there any investments/shares/ISAs/Premium Bonds that need to be shut down or transferred?

Insurance Was there any life insurance? If so, for whom and for how much?

Pension Was there a private pension in place that can be transferred? Was there a company pension?

Tax Do you need to gather what you need to be able to fill in a tax return? Can you do this yourself or do you need an accountant?

Accountancy Did the person already have an accountant? If not, do you need to find one or can you do it yourself?

Work
Who you need to tell:
Employers
Employees
Contractors
Suppliers
Clients

If the person was self-employed, were there business partners and if so do you need a corporate lawyer to help sell the deceased's share of the business or an adviser to help reorganise the business?

House
Is there a mortgage provider who needs to be informed?
If the house is rented, whose name is the tenancy in?
Are there others still living in the home and, if so, can they stay there?
Services such as gas, electricity and water may need to be informed or accounts transferred or shut down.
Insurance providers – car, house, travel, pets, possessions and so on – all need to be informed.

If there is a car, whose name is it registered in? Will this need to be changed? What will the effects of this be on the insurance?

Parking permits may need to be transferred.

Council Tax will need to be informed.

Who will take care of any pets left behind?

Digital

Email accounts.

Online subscriptions – websites such as Spotify or Amazon.

Television and broadband providers such as Sky or Virgin and subscription channels such as Netflix or Now TV.

Mobile phone providers.

TV licence.

Other

Gym memberships.

Club memberships.

Magazine or newspaper subscriptions.

As you can see, there are a lot of people who may be affected by the death and you may come across many others in the course of negotiating all the above issues.

However, most companies have a bereavement department who are trained both in shutting down accounts and in knowing how to treat a bereaved person with respect and care. So always try asking for this department first as it will reduce the number of times you have to repeat yourself, as well as minimising the chances of coming into contact with a 'jobsworth' who doesn't handle you gently enough.

Planning the funeral

This is a big one and I highly recommend asking a friend to help. I would also recommend taking advantage of many of the online funeral planner websites out there.

Some of the things you need to think about are:

- Finding a local funeral parlour – a good one will be invaluable in helping you navigate this whole process.

- You can find a registered one via the National Association of Funeral Directors (nafd.org.uk).

- What type of service do you want – religious or secular?

- Who will lead the service – a religious leader or a humanist celebrant or a friend?

- Where will it take place?

- Will there be a burial or a cremation?

- Will there be a smaller family service for the burial or cremation and a larger one for a bigger friendship group, or just one for everyone? If separate, will these be on the same day or on different days and which will come first?

- Who will write and deliver the eulogies and obituaries (this doesn't have to be the same person if the best writer is not necessarily the best speaker).

- Will you have songs and music? Will these be live or from recordings? Do you need an organist or other musicians? A choir? A sound system?

- Will there be poetry or readings and if so, who might be appropriate to read them?

- Who will write and organise the printing of the Order of Service?

- Do you want to include photos or a slideshow, or decorate the room in some other way?

- Will you provide food and drink afterwards – if so, where and for how many?

- Who will carry the coffin?

- How will you pay for the funeral?

- Will you be accepting flowers and if so, where should they be sent?

- If not, perhaps you might like to ask for donations to a favourite charity. You will need to think about how best to accept these donations if so.

- Is there a dress code?

- Is there parking or public transport information you need to give people?

How will you be travelling to the funeral, and who will accompany the hearse?

Do you need ushers? Do you need a seating plan?

These are just a few examples of the sort of decisions that will crop up for you.

Arranging probate

Probate is the process that you need to go through for the will to be accepted as valid or – when there is no will – for the estate to be settled via the intestacy process.

You can arrange this yourself and there is online support to help you through it, or you can find a local probate lawyer to do it for you.

Be warned, though, whether you do it yourself or have a lawyer do it, this can be a rather lengthy and admin-heavy process and will nearly always take far longer than you anticipate. And many decisions cannot be taken until probate is granted, so start the process as soon as you can.

Going back to work

- Take as much time off as your employer's compassionate leave policy allows.

- If your inclination is to rush back to the distraction of work as soon as possible, remember grief is a long, slow process; please treat yourself gently and understand that coping with a bereavement is a marathon not a sprint.

- Identify your most trusted colleague, who can pass on the news to others in advance if you feel worried about having to tell multiple people in person.

- Let that designated person know what and how much information you are happy to divulge and whether you welcome questions or not.

- If you would prefer not to have to talk about it in the work environment then let this person know just how much acknowledgement you feel able to manage so they can pass this information on as well.

Sorting out possessions

When and how to sort and clear out 'stuff' is a really difficult and personal decision. Sometimes your situation will mean you don't have much choice, but if you do have any say in the matter I would advise not to do too much too soon, as you may change your mind as to what is necessary or unnecessary to keep. I found it very hard to make any changes at all in the first year, and when I did I found it a very upsetting process, so pick your days and times wisely and perhaps have a trusted person with you.

If you have the space and no pressing need to remove things and prefer to keep hold of as much as you can, then do that. There are no rules here – getting rid of things doesn't 'mean' anything about where you are with your grief, just as hanging on to things doesn't need to be symbolic of anything either. You do what is right for you, and don't let anyone persuade you otherwise.

Triggers

The smallest thing can act as a trigger back into another period of intense grief. It may be a smell, a piece of music, a phrase someone uses, an advert for a particular product, an item on a menu, a visit to a place that you only ever went to together before. These can catch you off guard, trigger flashbacks, and plunge you unexpectedly back into a place of deep emotion, long after you thought the worst was over. It is upsetting and you will probably feel as though you have taken a huge step backward, but remember that grief is a series of waves, and that just because you may temporarily feel like no time at all has passed and you will never get through it, you have before and you will again. Triggers do keep coming I'm afraid and when they do they are awful and frightening, but they do seem to get fewer and further between as time goes on.

I remember feeling furious with people who would tell me that 'time heals' because it felt so dismissive of my experience and my relationship with Bill, as if all it needed was for time to pass and for him to recede into memory and I would be 'healed'. I didn't want to be healed; I didn't want to forget him. And yet I did want the pain to stop. And now I see that both those things can be true. I can be feeling a lot 'better' a lot of the time, but it doesn't mean I am healed. It's like having a wound that will always be there, but of which I am not massively conscious, most of the time. I have learned to live with it, and it stays quiet and not at the forefront of my mind. But occasionally some trigger will prod that bruise, open up the wound and remind me how much it hurts. So, I don't think that it is true to say time heals exactly, but time does provide the opportunity to let the wound scab over, so it is less raw. Triggers rip that scab off and it bleeds again for a while, but that just means you need to tend to it gently and make sure it has the opportunity to scab over again, forming that extra layer of protection, to make it more liveable-with once more.

Anniversaries

Anniversaries – birthdays, the date of the death, wedding anniversaries, Mother's Day, Father's Day – all carry huge potential to trigger you back into a dark place; but at least, on some level, they are expected and can be prepared for. Not that that makes them less painful, but you can at least identify them more easily.

Weirdly, even if your conscious mind has forgotten an anniversary of some sort, your unconscious will often remind you. I find that a couple of weeks before Bill's or my dad's birthdays, and the anniversaries of their deaths, I start to feel achy, tired and depressed. I start to wonder why I feel like this before registering which date is approaching, then it makes sense. This is a common phenomenon among grievers.

It is also absolutely okay to ignore these dates completely if you would rather not engage, and sometimes you may even really forget them; or you may just feel nothing around them. To many, after all, it is only a date, and not everyone reacts or feels they can emote 'to order' around a calendar date.

Or you might see these dates as extra opportunities to celebrate the life of your dead loved one, to organise a party in their honour, get the photos out, or use it as an excuse to get together to remember them and go over old memories.

Something that can make anniversaries hard is the reaction – or non-reaction – of other people. Some friends and family may want to make a big thing of the date, and have a big get-together, which can be really hard when you would rather just have a day alone, or if you want the day to pass without comment. Other friends may not even remember that it is a significant date, which may be upsetting if you do want to celebrate or commemorate it. As always, it is not only ourselves and our own grief that needs managing, it is how that interacts with others who were close to the dead person, and you may all be at very different places with this.

See earlier on creating a legacy for potential ways to mark the occasion, if you choose to mark it.

Christmas

Christmas is of course one anniversary that none of us are ever likely to forget. Whether you generally love Christmas or hate it, if someone significant to you has died it is going to be painful for so many reasons:

You are hit very squarely in the face not only with the loss of the person, but with the routines and traditions of a day that for most has a rhythm and a shape that rarely changes over the course of a lifetime. Now it will have to. There will be a huge loved-one-shaped hole in the putting up of the tree, the opening of the presents, the arrangements for getting to or preparing to greet the family members you normally spend the days with.

It highlights their absence and can make you feel even more isolated.

It is a time when we are 'meant' to be happy and joyful and celebratory – and are bombarded with images and messages telling us that other people are so (the secret is that they're not most of the time, but that doesn't stop the relentless propaganda).

Nowadays Christmas is not just a day but weeks of relentless forced jollity, leaving no room for real life nor space to grieve.

Your everyday routines that may have become lifelines will be shaken up.

You may be having to reject invitations to parties and nights out that you have no interest in, or you may feel you have to attend yet feel miserable at each one, or exhausted from having to keep the sociable mask in place.

Many of your support networks – friends or having work to go to – are all unavailable as everything shuts down and friends either leave town to see their own families or are closeted in their own homes and it feels wrong to disturb them at this family time.

You may feel the need to pretend to be 'okay' even more than normal, either because you don't want to bring down the prevailing mood, or because you have children or other family members for whom you want to make it 'nice', and so you strap the mask on even more firmly, burying your real feelings even deeper than normal. This is not helpful to either them or you, though.

This is particularly true if you are with children who are grieving someone significant. Your instinct may be to try to give them a fantastic Christmas filled with joy to make up for the fact that they have had a pretty rough year thus far. But remember that feeling sad is not something to jolly them out of or suppress.

It may only confuse them, or shame them, if they are sad when everyone around them is telling them it is a time of joy. It is important to acknowledge that Christmas can be difficult as well and that if they don't feel like entering into the spirit, that is fine too. The best present you can give them is not to pretend – which only forces them to pretend too – but to remain honest about how it's okay to enjoy Christmas, but also okay to still be sad or angry at times too. A 'great' or 'perfect' Christmas is not going to make up for the bad year that preceded it, so don't try to make it so. If all the family genuinely want to celebrate and 'forget' for a day, however, then of course go with that. There are no rules here, and no one way to manage Christmas.

The supposedly festive time is likely to be painful one way or another, but there are a few strategies you might adopt depending on your preference, the phase of your grief, and the needs of the rest of the family:

- **Avoidance** My own preferred method is to run away to a foreign, hotter country where Christmas does not figure so large in the culture and I can do something active with strangers, like yoga or cycling. This running-away option is a good opportunity to be in company, but not in a Christmassy way, as it will likely bring you into contact with other people who are also trying to avoid remembering that it's Christmas.

- **Change the routine** Shake up all the traditions that you would have normally indulged in. Go to a different family member's house, do the present-opening at the opposite end of the day, eat the meal at a different time, 'adopt' a refugee family or an elderly couple for the day. Ask every family member to nominate a new activity or habit that can, over the years, become a new tradition.

Keep the routine Conversely, you could keep the routines exactly the same and keep a space alive for your dead loved one. You can reminisce about the other Christmases and what the person would be saying or doing at any one point. You can keep a candle burning – literally and/or metaphorically – and be very aware and conscious of them all day. You can ask other family members to take on the various roles your person would have done and talk about them constantly.

Honour them Create a new ritual that keeps their memory present – find a new tree decoration to represent them, put out a new photo – tinsel-draped or not – drink a toast with their favourite drink, cook their favourite meal, hang them out a stocking, keep their place at the table, make a donation to their favourite charity, sing their favourite carol. Celebrate the fact that you had them for the years that you had them, rather than only mourning the fact that they have gone.

Work Having contact with others who are not family members can be helpful. If you work in a job that requires someone to do the Christmas shift, then offering to do this will make you very popular with colleagues who don't want to throw their hat in the ring, it will earn you extra money, and most importantly it will give you something to do that will occupy your brain and allow you to forget what day it is, for a while at least. Remember that distraction can often be a useful, if short-term, strategy.

- **Volunteer** Many homeless and refugee charities, some care homes, some animal charities if you prefer to avoid humans, are generally delighted to welcome volunteers. You can work with those who perhaps don't have much choice about where to spend the day, who would not otherwise have a warm meal, or a roof over their head, or even the opportunity to chat with a kind person to help them through. Many people – and not only grievers – do this year after year and love the opportunity to have fun, meet new people, and feel they are giving back. It won't be for everyone, and if you are in the very early days of grieving it might even be too depressing, but most of the time a real effort is made to keep the mood light and sociable. Do look into this very far ahead however as demand to volunteer can be high, and most places will want to offer you some training in advance.

Whichever strategy you adopt it is important to:

- Plan ahead

- Adjust your expectations as to what Christmas 'should' look like.

- Know that you can say no to offers from others – and to say no to 'well-meaning' advice that doesn't land well too.

- Know that you can ask for what you need.

- Know that the Samaritans are open twenty-four hours a day, 365 days a year and will be happy to talk to you any time over the festive period if you feel really low.

- All the suggestions in this book hold true, and are possibly more important than ever, at Christmas. So above all else be mindful of what you eat and drink and don't overindulge, attend to your self-care, get out into the fresh air, do some exercise, don't ignore the sad moments, don't feel guilty over the happy moments, and try to keep in contact with trusted friends.

- Remember other family members who are also grieving will not necessarily be grieving in the same way as you and you may all approach Christmas differently. Be as gentle as you can with each other in negotiating these differing needs.

What to Do When Life Keeps Happening?

Christmas, birthdays, any sort of anniversary; all these dates provide very obvious markers in the sand. It becomes impossible to ignore the fact that time is passing, which might prompt more existential reflection on where you are and on what has happened or not happened since the death. It might feel like the opening of a new chapter and lead to a taking-stock, or to the making of resolutions. And at the same time you will constantly be bombarded by time's very relentless habit of marching on regardless. It will continually bring unfolding new situations, all of which have the potential to bring more grief issues in their wake. Many life-changing events could happen to throw you off course:

- You may be grieving a partner but starting to wonder what it might be like to start dating again.

- You may want to have sex again.

- You may be grieving a child but be wondering whether to have another one, or may accidentally be expecting another one, or a friend may be expecting a new baby.

- You may be grieving a friend and one day realise you have forgotten their anniversary or birthday.

- Your dead friend's partner may have met someone new and you feel conflicted about whether it's okay to like that new person.

- Your bereaved parent may have met someone new.

- Your friends may have stopped talking about or asking about your grief or about your person.

- You may need to change job or house and so feel you are in danger of forgetting your person if you're no longer in the place you most associate with them.

These are just some of the very many complicated, multifaceted, contradictory-emotion-provoking happenings that will – that have to – happen. These are hard but unstoppable new milestones to encounter and cope with. Remember that research has found that many people manage to have a continuing relationship with their dead loved one; and that such an internalised relationship can adapt and respond to new situations and life events, just as the relationship would have continued to develop had the person lived. A relationship is dynamic and evolving and can be so in death as in life. So please try to take your loved one with you into your new reality, knowing they want the best for you, however challenging that may sometimes be.

Remember too that in your constantly evolving relationship with your grief and with your dead loved one, you are allowed to change your mind. You are allowed to say that things are getting harder before they get easier, or that new situations are evoking different sorts of challenges that require different recalibrations.

An incident such as meeting a potential new partner after losing a spouse may on the surface bring great joy. But it might be tinged with many other emotions as well. It will not be uncomplicated. You may have thought long and hard about starting a new relationship. You may intellectually decide you are ready and that years have passed, only to find that the minute you embark on something, emotionally you are far from ready. Suddenly you feel like you are having an affair and it is as though no time at all has passed and your loss happened all of a week ago. Time can really telescope to and fro. In all of this, go gently, keep checking in with yourself, keep breathing and keep being self-compassionate.

For Friends of Grieving Friends

In *Languages of Loss* I included some ideas as to how to support a grieving friend. It is the part of the book that is most often quoted back to me as being the most useful.

I therefore would like to refer back to some of those suggestions, and add a few more, because if you are a friend who would like to help, you are going to play a massively important role and I understand that it can be hard to know how to help.

Be there

This is the most important thing of all. Don't worry about 'getting it wrong' or not knowing what to say. None of us do. There isn't really anything to say beyond acknowledging that a terrible thing has happened and that you are there for them.

Allow for the contradictions

Your friend is cycling through an overwhelming mix of emotions at great pace, so don't expect consistency. Go with the flow – comfort when that is what feels needed, indulge the denial and need for humour if that is more to the fore. Chat when they want to chat, stay quiet but present when they seem exhausted. Communicate. Listen. Let them talk.

Don't fire questions at them

They probably don't know the answer. Make it plain they can tell or ask you anything when the need arises, but don't expect them to always know what they want or need. Try to just read the ever-changing mood.

Follow don't lead

Don't assume you know what is right for them or tell them to do their grief differently. Allow them to do it their way and don't try to control them. That includes not telling them to be strong, nor telling them to feel it 'more'. Don't even praise them for 'doing well', just let them be how they are minute by minute.

Don't judge

Their way may not be your way but you are not them and cannot know what is behind their behaviours. They are not necessarily fully themselves at this time and are just doing what they can to get by. Try to be compassionate about this even if you disapprove.

Know what you're good at

- If it is listening, then offer that and gently encourage them to talk about the person who has died.

- If it is talking then tell them stories and memories about the person.

- If you are emotional and likely to get upset, then offer practical support.

- Compile a list of tasks and sign up volunteers for each.

- Find someone who can move in on the nights the grieving friend doesn't want to be alone.

- Identify the insomniacs who could receive phone calls in the early hours when the night terrors strike.

- Find a practical person who is willing to cook and clean.

- Find a good organiser to help plan the funeral.

- Find an efficient person to help deal with probate and other paperwork.

- Spread the word, cancel the griever's work and other commitments, think of ways to keep them gently occupied when needed – go walking with them, offer them your dog to cuddle, suggest books, podcasts, TV shows.

Help with finances

This can be a sensitive area, and many people will not want you to be involved, or even to discuss it. Obviously respect their privacy if so. But some people are plunged into financial difficulties if they have lost a spouse who was a breadwinner, if they have lost the carer's allowance they relied on, if they are too traumatised to work, or for a myriad other reasons. If you suspect the death has left them vulnerable financially then you may want to consider asking other friends to start a fund for them. This could be used either to pay for the funeral or just to keep them afloat, or in time, for therapeutic support or a holiday.

Don't take it personally

Any anger, rejection or lack of interest coming your way is the grief expressing itself. Try not to react or take it personally, just let the person know that you are still there for them when they want you to be. Similarly, if they rebuff early advances try again later, as they may be more able to receive help weeks or months down the line. Don't overdo it though; they may genuinely not want your help and you don't want to hassle. Just a gentle reminder that you are there from time to time should be enough.

Look after yourself

Read the sections on nurturing and self-compassion and make sure you do the same for yourself.

Don't be fooled by the 'mask'

They may well be looking like they are 'doing well' – and they probably are – but that doesn't mean that they have forgotten, moved on, or that they are not still thinking about the person and suffering.

Don't be fooled by time

It is not just the first two years or so that are difficult. It will continue to be difficult for many years to come. Don't assume that just because much time has passed, or because your friend often seems happy and to have 'moved on', that new life events are not evoking all sorts of issues below the surface. Tread gently and don't mistake the surface presentation for the whole story.

Don't stop

Months and years later the grief will have changed shape, but it won't have gone completely. Keep checking in, keep sending messages of support, keep talking about the person.

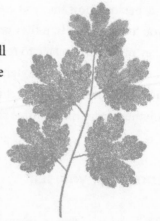

Epilogue

I finished writing *Languages of Loss* roughly fourteen months after Bill's death. It minutely chronicles those awful, painful months filled with all their acute shock and terror. As I wrote of my pain, I was worried I wouldn't know how to end that part of my story, given that grief doesn't end. Yet as I approached what became my closing pages and looked back to what I had written at the start, I could clearly see that I was in a very different place fourteen months on. I had found moments of hope and lightness in among the misery and pain, and I was more optimistic about my future, ready to embark on the next unknowable – and unwritten – chapter. Those changes had been almost imperceptible to perceive while they were happening and could only be discerned from a distance.

Your own evolving shifts in perspective may feel similarly non-existent and impossible to you now, no matter how many of my 'suggestions' you attempt. It may be that that immersion, that inability to see a way out, is a necessary part of the journey.

I have been writing *A Grief Companion* over the course of the subsequent fourteen months, and as I find myself again contemplating how to end it, I have been reflecting on how differently I feel again now, two and half years on from Bill's death.

For a start, I can see that it has felt quite natural to write of my own experience in the past tense. I can look back at how I felt just after Bill's death as a period that has ended, even while my grief itself hasn't ended. It has certainly changed flavour and intensity, however. Of course, sometimes I am dunked right back under those stormy waves, but generally my grief manifests more manageably and less intrusively. It could even be true to say that my grief has itself become a 'companion' of sorts, albeit a companion with whom I have wrestled, and who I tried hard to conquer and banish. Yet that very wrestling has led us, my grief and I, into an intimate relationship of mutual understanding, respect and even love. Now I wouldn't want to be without this valuable companion who reminds me daily of how much I love and miss Bill, and who has taught me so much about myself, and about life. And death. When I discussed this notion with a widower friend of mine, he said that he similarly did not see his grief as only negative. He felt it supporting him like an invisible arm around his shoulder.

I can't pretend that the second year involved a steady upward progression towards feeling more at ease with and welcoming of my grief. No, it has been an unyielding struggle towards compromise, an exhausting game of give and take, and on occasion this new phase has felt harder than the first. During the first year my pain was acute, everything was new and to a certain extent I was living off adrenaline and a desire to power on through. Just when I thought I was getting a handle on how to manage life, the second year brought a more chronic pain and the inescapable knowledge of my aloneness. Reality hit me over the head with all its unrelenting mundanity and that brought a real trudge through suffering of a different magnitude.

However, more recent months have brought a third and again different phase. The majority of this book has been written during the Covid-19 lockdown with all its crazy upside down-ness, much of which mirrored my early grief and on occasion plunged me back there. Yet it was also perversely comforting and I felt less alone in many ways. I felt as though the rest of the world could now understand better what it is like to have your world upended and your future uncertain. I took no pleasure in this recognition, but I did feel more understood. In other ways lockdown was terrifying and made me confront my loneliness head on as I spent night after night alone in my house wishing Bill was here to share it with me.

Languages of Loss was published in the second week of lockdown. All the in-person launch events and exciting publication publicity were cancelled in the wake of Covid-19 but I found myself instead being asked to write articles about lockdown-related grief and mourning, and to do some online interviews on the subject. While I was of course delighted to be asked and hoped that I might have something vaguely useful to contribute to these frightening times, I did find myself slightly disconcerted by the nature of the questioning. Over and over again I would be asked for my 'top five ways' to manage grief, or for my 'one essential piece of advice' to help those bereaved by Covid-19. Everyone wanted to know 'what should I do?' and 'how can I stop the pain?'

These were of course impossible questions to answer. There is no easy summing up of how to make it less painful. No one wants to hear the inescapable truth – that grief is painful and undergoing it during a pandemic is only going to bring up yet more complications. I had just published a 263-page book explaining just how complex and unavoidable grief is and how the only way through it is through it – yet everyone wanted the in-a-nutshell formula. In *Languages of Loss* I had recounted how it was for me, and asked people to explore how it was for them. I had detailed the reality of grief being un-sum-up-able or boil down-able into a neat list and yet now I was seeing that this neatness is what people really desire. I of course understand that search for easy answers and that desperate desire for shortcuts. *A Grief Companion* is in many ways a response to that need for a helping hand. Sadly I can't take the pain away for you. I can't even offer a handy five-point checklist. I certainly can't give you my one essential top tip. I wish I could. Instead all I can offer is to share with you some more of my thoughts and learnings about what made each day a tiny bit more bearable for me. I pray that some of those learnings will occasionally help you too.

Resources

This is far from being a comprehensive list of anything. It is a very personal list offering some pointers towards books, websites, podcasts and organisations that you may or may not find useful to explore. Please feel free to ask others for the people and places they found useful, and do get in touch if you want to suggest what has been helpful to you.

Books about bereavement

That I have read and 'enjoyed':

No Death, No Fear by Thich Nhat Hanh (Buddhist perspective I found rather comforting)

The Year of Magical Thinking by Joan Didion (about the death of both her partner and her child. Good description of how disorientating grief can be but quite dense and literary)

A Grief Observed by C. S. Lewis (about the death of his wife, made into the film *Shadowlands*. Also a reflection on how his Christianity was shaken, then restored, by his experience)

All at Sea by Decca Aitkenhead (journalist whose husband died by drowning)

Grief Works by Julia Samuel (not a personal memoir but very good on the experience of grief, written by a therapist working in the area for twenty-five years and including case studies of some of her clients)

The Journey from Abandonment to Healing by Susan Anderson (not specifically about bereavement, but loss of any relationship)

Insomniac City by Bill Hayes (only rather tangentially about bereavement but an interesting read nonetheless)

Grief is the Thing With Feathers by Max Porter (a novel rather than a factual account, but great if you like seeing the world through metaphor)

H is for Hawk by Helen Macdonald (oblique but beautiful memoir about the training of a hawk as a response to her father's death)

Proof of Heaven by Eben Alexander (about the existence of life after death by a neuroscientist – not for everyone!)

The Five People You Meet In Heaven by Mitch Albom

Staring at the Sun by Irvin Yalom (psychotherapist and author exploring fear of death – his own and that of his clients)

Badger's Parting Gifts by Susan Varley (for kids but actually quite lovely for adults too)

Michael Rosen's Sad Book by Michael Rosen (looks like it should be a kids' book but is definitely aimed at adults too)

These next few have been recommended to me by others, but I don't have personal experience of them:

Life After You by Lucie Brownlee

I Wasn't Ready to Say Goodbye by Blake Noel

'You'll Get Over It': The Rage of Bereavement by Virginia Ironside

When Bad Things Happen to Good People by Harold Kushner

Through Grief by Elizabeth Collick

The Courage to Grieve by Judy Tatelbaum

Healing Grief by Barbara Ward
The Early Days of Grieving by Derek Nuttall
Time Lived, Without its Flow by Denise Riley
A Widow's Story: A Memoir by Joyce Carol Oates
A Manual for Heartache by Cathy Rentzenbrink
Sex After Grief: Navigating Your Sexuality After Losing Your Beloved by Joan Price
Everyday Madness by Lisa Appignanesi
Dying, Death and Grief by Brenda Mallon
The Mindful Path to Self-Compassion by Christopher K. Germer
Start Where You Are: A Guide to Compassionate Living by Pema Chödrön
Finding What You Didn't Lose by John Fox
It's OK That You're Not OK by Megan Devine
Motherless Daughters by Hope Edelman
The Last Days of Rabbit Hayes by Anna McPartlin (fiction)
Mindfulness & the Journey of Bereavement by Peter Bridgewater

Academic books aimed mainly at therapists but which may be useful and of interest to non-therapists:
On Grief and Grieving by Elisabeth Kübler-Ross and David Kessler
Collected Works, vol 14, Mourning and Melancholia by Sigmund Freud
Continuing Bonds – New Understandings of Grief, Klass, Silverman and Nickman (eds.)
The Other Side of Sadness by George Bonanno
Bearing the Unbearable by Joanne Cacciatore

Other potentially useful and interesting books:
The Body Keeps the Score by Bessel van der Kolk
The Body Remembers by Babette Rothschild
Breathe by Jean Hall

How to find a therapist

UK Council for Psychotherapy (psychotherapy.org.uk)
British Association for Counselling and Psychotherapy
  (bacp.co.uk)
Counselling Directory (counselling-directory.org.uk)

Support groups, websites, communities etc

untanglegrief.com
Online community matching the bereaved with those who can support – as friends and mentors, as well as with professionals who can help with practicalities. They also offer online practical guides.

thegoodgriefproject.co.uk
Supporting families after the untimely death of a loved one, particularly a child; encouraging creative ways to engage with grief; and promoting understanding around what it means to grieve in a society that doesn't like to talk about it.

cruse.org.uk
A charity offering free bereavement counselling by volunteers. They also provide free booklets and factsheets online.

deathcafe.com

Cafes where you can talk with others about anything death-related.

widowedandyoung.org.uk

Also known as WAY, this is a charity and support group for those widowed under the age of fifty.

griefencounter.org.uk

Grief support for bereaved children and young people.

lifedeathwhatever.com

A death doula and a funeral director attempt to redesign the conversation around death and dying.

thegoodgrieftrust.org

Offering support to the bereaved, by the bereaved.

childbereavementuk.org

For bereaved children, or families who have experienced the death of a child.

Podcasts:

Grief Works
Griefcast
On the Marie Curie Couch
What's Your Grief
Shapes of Grief
Grief Encounters
Grief Is My Superpower

Acknowledgements

Many incredible people have been my own grief companions. They have gone above and beyond in their generous provision of support, comfort, fun, humour and acres of their time and love. They have given me reasons to keep going when those reasons have been hard to find alone. I cannot thank them enough and know that a mention in this book is scant compensation for all that they have done, particularly during this year of lockdown when they have also been battling their own demons.

From the bottom of my heart, I would like to offer my love, thanks, admiration and undying friendship to (in alphabetical order because that's the only fair way) Joanne Admiraal, Julia Cooke, Libby Davies, Katie Dias, Jess Fawkes, Sarah Fielding, Tamsin Greig, Louise Hooper, Tanya Hudson, Ian Leese, Paul Moreton, David Murray, Lucy Payne, Sherie Ryder, Inge Samuels, Peter Sweasey and Francesca Urquhart.

For reading portions of this book, offering invaluable advice, some of it the result of your own deep and painful contact with grief, and just for being great friends, I would like to thank Julia Cooke (again), Emma Garrett, Julian Mayers, Lizzie Pickering, Nicole Scott, and Peter Sweasey (again).

For making me feel so welcome in my new home and listening to me talk so much and so often about Billy, whom you never even met, thank you to new and lovely friends, Kate van Beek, Charlie Severs, Susi Venables and Rima Williams.

For aiding and abetting me in keeping Billy's name alive in both the private and the public spheres, thank you to the Charlton, Rowe and Cashmore families, Pip Bergin, Chris Bilton, Broo Doherty, Simon Marlow, Tim Marlow, Mike Sims, Simon Snashall, Julia Sowerbutts, Anya Woolliams and all the staff at the Lyric Theatre, Hammersmith.

For sharing your yogic and life wisdom, as well as for her valued friendship, thank you Zephyr Wildman.

For support, guidance and friendship, thank you Hammersmith Quakers.

For unremitting support and love, thanks to my mother and fellow widow, Ellie Bates.

And finally, a massive thank you to those without whom this book, nor *Languages of Loss*, would have been possible – my wonderful agent Jane Graham Maw and to all at Yellow Kite, especially Liz Gough, Emma Knight and Jacqui Lewis.

About the Author

Sasha Bates is a psychotherapist, writer and former documentary filmmaker. Eighteen years in the TV industry saw her write, direct and produce series as varied as Omnibus, Grand Designs, Live and Kicking and How to Look Good Naked, alongside on-going sidelines in travel journalism and yoga teaching.

Her fascination with people – with what makes us tick and what creates the myriad dynamics between us all – fuelled this first career as a filmmaker and led to her going even deeper with her second career as a psychotherapist. Having gained an MA and advanced diploma in integrative psychotherapy from The Minster Centre in London she worked in the NHS and in higher education before setting up her own private practice.

When her husband, Bill Cashmore, died unexpectedly at just fifty-six, Sasha turned back to writing to help her make sense of the tumultuous feelings of grief that were overwhelming her. As she wrote her pain onto the page, she found her therapist self entering the conversation, using therapeutic theory to help her navigate through the new and unwelcome world into which she had been thrust. Her first book – *Languages of Loss* – was the result of that dual narrative approach. The feedback she received from this revealed how hungry people were for more direct and straightforward conversations about grief. *A Grief Companion*, her second book, aims to fill that gap and provide some practical tools to help grievers navigate this painful and confusing time.

Sasha continues to write, teaches workshops about grief to other grievers, and to other therapists, and has founded a commemorative theatrical bursary – The Bill Cashmore Award – in conjunction with the Lyric Theatre Hammersmith.

To find out more please visit **sashabates.co.uk**

@sashbates on Twitter, Instagram and Facebook.

Also by Sasha Bates

LANGUAGES OF LOSS
A psychotherapist's journey through grief

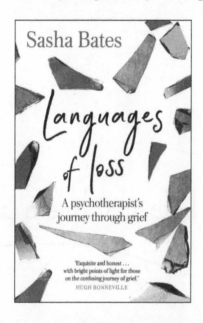

One person, two perspectives on grief. Plunged unexpectedly into widowhood at just 49 years old, psychotherapist Sasha Bates describes in searing honesty the agonisingly raw feelings unleashed by the loss of her husband and best friend, Bill. At the same time, she attempts to keep her therapist hat in place and create some perspective from psycho-analytic theory. From the depths of her confusion she gropes for ways to manage and bear the pain – by looking back at all that she has learnt from psychotherapeutic research, and from accepted grief theories, to help her make sense of her altered reality.

Paperback 978 1 529 31716 9

books to help you live a good life

Join the conversation and tell
us how you live a #goodlife

🐦 @yellowkitebooks
f YellowKiteBooks
P Yellow Kite Books
📷 YellowKiteBooks